THE WITCH'S ALMANAC 2006

THE WITCH'S ALMANAC 2006

Practical Magic and Spells for Every Season

MARIE BRUCE

quantum

LONDON • NEW YORK • TORONTO • SYDNEY

quantum
An imprint of W. Foulsham and Co. Ltd
The Publishing House, Bennetts Close, Cippenham, Slough,
Berkshire, SL1 5AP, England

ISBN 0-572-03133-6

Cover illustration by Jurgen Ziewe

A CIP record for this book is available from the British Library

Neither the editors of W. Foulsham & Co. Ltd nor the author nor the publisher take responsibility for any possible consequences from any treatment, procedure, test, exercise, action or application of medication or preparation by any person reading or following the information in this book. In particular, herbal or aromatic preparations should be avoided during pregnancy.

Always take the greatest care when using candles and follow safety advice given in this book. Always fix a candle in an appropriate holder and make sure it is not placed next to anything flammable before lighting. Never leave a lighted candle unattended.

Printed in Great Britain by Creative Print and Design (Wales), Ebbw Vale

Contents

Introduction

During the passing of a single year, we all experience many changes, both good and bad. Just as the cycle of nature rolls from one season to the next, so there is a seasonal pattern in our lives; learning how to recognise and use these seasonal phases is a fundamental key to magical living. None of us knows what the new year holds in store ... marriage or divorce, births or deaths, unemployment or career advancement, health or illness, poverty or prosperity – these are just some of the things that touch all of our lives at some point or other. But the truth is that it's not what life throws at us that counts; it's how we deal with it.

I have no idea what the next 12 months will bring into your life or mine, but I do know that positive attitude and preparation are vital. There is substance and meaning to the old saying, 'Hope for the best, prepare for the worst'. Although we can all be caught off guard on occasion – those bad times when life throws us a fire ball and expects us to catch it – if we consistently work to strengthen our defences and maintain a positive attitude, we maximise our chances of success at the game of life.

Within the pages of this book are spells for every week of the year, as well as rituals and exercises to help you attune with the seasons. You will find in-depth information about the concepts of the Craft, astrological signs, magical correspondences, moon phases and positive life skills, plus details of witches' tools, Circle-castings and how to create your own unique altars and Book of Shadows.

Witchcraft isn't just for Halloween; it's a way of life, a daily discovery, and those of you who take the time to study this book and put its concepts into practice will reap the rewards and live magically. The universe always pays its debts, so if you can smile through the bad times, your courage will be rewarded. If you can wipe away someone's tears while hiding your own, that selfless act will be recognised. And if during your day, you can make one person laugh, that day will not have been wasted.

I hope the year to come brings you all that you could wish for, and as little sorrow as possible. The purpose of *The Witch's Almanac* is to help you re-discover the beauty of nature and the magic of the Craft. Contained within this book are the intimate secrets of my personal strength, the kind of magic I make and the magical skills that have helped me through the darker days. May they work as well for you.

Bright blessings

Morgana

About Witches and Witchcraft

As modern life runs at an ever more frantic pace, many of us choose to look to the ancient wisdom of nature for lessons in how to slow down, relax, step back and escape. You cannot rush the seasons or hurry the growth of a tree. Just as 'time and tide wait for no man', so too do 'little acorns mighty oak trees make'. Both proverbs illustrate that nature has always gone at its own pace and always will. If we are to live a magical life, we need to attune ourselves to this pace, as magic and witchcraft are deeply rooted in nature.

As witches, we honour the passing of the seasons, holding special celebrations and rituals to mark these transitional times in the year. These celebrations are known as sabbats. There are eight of them in all, and collectively they are known to pagans as the wheel of the year. The sabbats help us to keep a grip on the natural world, to harness its magic and to dance with the rhythms of life. In this book we will discuss each of them, together with its particular traditions and some of the deities associated with it.

Witchcraft is one of the best things that's ever happened to me – it's right up there with falling in love, seeing my name in print for the first time and my first gallop on a horse when I was 10! Hopefully, by the end of this book, it will be one of the best things that's ever happened to you too. I have practised the Craft for many years now, and it has helped me to achieve balance in my life and make my dreams come true. I feel very honoured and privileged to be able to teach others about the wonderful gift that is magic.

If you have read my previous books (see page 224), you will already have a firm foundation of Craft knowledge to build upon. If you are new to the Craft, however, this book will serve as an introduction and will be your guide as you take your first steps on the magical path. Here you will learn not only what witches do but also how and why we do it – why we celebrate the turning of the seasons, which deities we call upon at particular times of the year, how we actually cast spells, and so on.

Whether you are an adept or neophyte witch, within these pages you will find spell-castings and rituals to both interest and challenge you. You will learn how to create potions, divine the future and choose for your work the crystals, trees, flowers and herbs appropriate to each month. Whatever the new year has in store for you – be it marriage, children, a new job or whatever – you will find spells in this book to suit your circumstances.

Concepts of the Craft

As I mentioned earlier, witchcraft is a practice based on a foundation of reverence for the natural world around us. As such, it is important to witches that we keep a firm grip on what is going on in the environment, particularly when it comes to the seasons, moon phases, days of the week and even weather. All these things are of vital importance when it comes to spell-casting – and as you've probably guessed, magical spells are an inherent part of the Craft.

Perhaps one of the most surprising thing about witches is that we believe that the higher power, or divinity, has both masculine and feminine aspects. Simply put, we believe in a goddess as well as a god, and many witches focus more strongly on the Goddess, who is seen as the mother of all life, and is also known as Mother Nature. This again illustrates what an important role nature plays in the practice of witchcraft.

While a detailed explanation of the Goddess and God is beyond the scope of this book, the following descriptions should serve to give newcomers to the Craft a better understanding of the role they play in the sacred craft of Wicca. When you begin to invoke particular deities, you will need to read up on their associations and attributes so that you have a sound knowledge of what you are invoking. There are many books available on this subject – you will find a selection in the New Age or Religions section of any major bookshop and in most large libraries.

The Goddess

The Goddess is probably the oldest deity there is. She has been worshipped in many cultures and has been called by many different names. To witches, the Goddess is strongly associated with the moon, and as such she has three aspects, collectively referred to as the Triple Goddess.

The first aspect of the Triple Goddess is known as the Maiden. Hers are the times of the new and waxing moon, the dawn and the spring. She stands for youth, freshness, births, new beginnings, seductions and enchantments. Her colour is white, symbolising innocence, purity and virginity.

It is worth mentioning here that in ancient times the word 'virgin' had an entirely different meaning from the modern one. Rather than denoting a woman who has never had sex, it indicated a woman who was beholden to no man – in short, a strong individual who went her own way and would not be ruled by masculine authority, although she might choose to take a partner and indulge in the pleasures of sex – the virgin goddess Diana, for example, had a deep passion for Endymion. In witchcraft we hold steady to the older meaning of the word virgin.

Women who have been raped or sexually abused may find this ancient meaning of the word very comforting, as it effectively signifies that we can all choose to be virgins! If virginity in its ancient context is a choice rather than a physical condition, it cannot be taken away or stolen from us by men. I feel that this is a very positive way to look at the word 'virginity' and, in turn, the power of choice and sexuality in women.

Several goddesses are known as representations of the Maiden Goddess: Diana, Artemis, Persephone and Maid Marian, for example. The virgin goddess of the moon and the hunt was known as Artemis to the Greeks and Diana to the Romans. Persephone, the Greek goddess of transformation and the spring, is especially powerful for those who have suffered loss, as she was abducted to the underworld by Hades, and allowed back to the Earth in spring for half the year. Maid Marian is also associated with spring.

Next comes the Mother aspect of the Goddess. There are many names for the Mother Goddess and she is perhaps the aspect most frequently called upon. She is the abundance of summer and the first fruitfulness of autumn. The main part of the day and the full moon are her times of power. She is loving and nurturing and offers gentle protection to those in need. She is creation, nature and Mother Earth. Her traditional colour is red, symbolising menstruation, birth and the blood of life.

There are many representations of the Mother Goddess. Gaia is the all-nourishing earth goddess; Aphrodite, the Greek goddess of love and passion; Ceres, the Roman goddess of fertility and abundance; Selene, the Greek goddess associated with fertility and intuitive power; Hera, the supreme Greek goddess of marriage and childbirth; Epona, the Gallic horse deity; and Gueniever (of the Arthurian legends), the goddess of love, growth and fertility.

The final aspect of the Triple Goddess is known as the Crone, or the Dark Mother. This is the Goddess most feared by those outside the Craft who have little understanding of Wiccan beliefs. The Crone is associated with death and the otherworld. Hers is the time of dusk and night, the waning and dark moon, autumn's end and the depths of winter. Her colour is black, which symbolises darkness, death and destruction, yet also protection and deep rest. She is the stereotypical hag - old, bent, fearsome and enshrouded in a dark cloak.

However, witches know that there is far more to the Crone than meets the eye, for she is the keeper of the mysteries and the mistress of all magic. She is wisdom and release, old age and rebirth, divination and prophecy. She has a powerful association with life and death. She brings justice in the form of karmic retribution to wrong-doers, and if you have need of her and can call on her without fear in your heart, she will provide powerful protection. I myself have called on the Dark Goddess for protection during a very difficult time and I have never felt more shielded and secure.

The Greek Hecate, goddess of the underworld, is a crone goddess with power to bring life from death. Kali is another incarnation, a Hindu goddess who can bring regeneration after sorrow. Other representations of the Dark Mother or Crone Goddess are: Branwen, the powerful Celtic goddess of love and beauty; Circe, goddess of the night; the Celtic mother goddess, Scota; the Celtic matron goddesses, the Morrigan and Morgan Le Fey.

The God

The first thing we need to clarify is that the witches' God is certainly not Satan or the devil. These manifestations of evil are Christian concepts and true witches don't even believe in their existence.

However, the God does bear some resemblance to the Christian devil, and the reason for this is that the practice of early Christianity evolved out of the old religion, Paganism. The early Christians imported many Pagan images into the new religion, one of which was the image of the Pagan God, which they turned into a symbol of evil. As Christianity grew and expanded, Pagans went into hiding and their goat-foot God went with them, leaving behind the Christian image of the devil, which was absorbed and developed in Christian culture.

Now, fortunately, people are less superstitious and far more informed than they once were, and Paganism in its many forms, Wicca included, has become one of the fastest-growing belief systems in the modern world. Bearing all that in mind, I'd say it's high time to re-evaluate the goat-foot God in his original form.

Like the Goddess, the God has many faces. In his most popular image he is half human and half beast, thus symbolising the fact that humans and animals are inter-connected and that the animal kingdom is equal and not inferior to human life, as many believe. In certain aspects, the God proudly sports a pair of antlers or horns on his brow. This, again, connects him to the animal kingdom, but more than that, the curve of the antler or horn symbolises the crescent moon, thus illustrating his union and association with the Goddess.

Although many witches focus mainly on the Goddess, we are always aware that the Goddess and God are equal. They are opposites, but they are also complementary, as both masculine and feminine are needed for life to take form and shape.

The God is associated with the sun and the heat of the summer. He is the strength of the mountains and the vastness of the sky. As the god of the harvest, or John Barleycorn, he is cut down in sacrifice each year, only to return with a new crop the following summer. The God is the protector of all animals, and he presides over sexual urges and procreation, which is especially evident in his aspect as Pan or the satyr. At the same time, the God is fun-loving, mischievous and a real party-goer, also being known as Lord of the Dance! He is loving and protective and is the wild force of vegetation and nature. In this aspect he is called Lord of the Greenwood, Lord of the Wildwood, Lord of the

Trees, Robin Hood, Herne the Hunter and the Green Man. Eros, Thor, Apollo, Adonis, Merlin, Odin, King Arthur, Osiris, Pan, Lancelot, Dionysus, Bacchus, Faunus and the goat-foot God are other names and faces of the witches' God.

Learning to know the gods

As you can see, there is more to the Goddess and the God than you may at first realise, and the aspects and names I have mentioned are just some of those that they go by. If you would like to delve deeper into the Goddess/God mysteries, then I suggest you read as much folklore and mythology as you can.

I must confess that during my first steps into the Craft, I left the God entirely alone. Although during my childhood I was not a regular church-goer, the only God I was aware of was the stern, judgemental Christian one. I felt quite uncomfortable at the idea of invoking a strange God I didn't know, and so I centred all my rituals and spell-castings on the Goddess. I probably would have gone on like this for a long time, had it not been for a very special dream.

I'd been having dreams of the Goddess for several weeks. My dream always took place in a forest, and the Goddess appeared as the epitome of feminine beauty, wearing a flowing white gown and a silver moon crown, and creating a shimmering light. On this particular occasion, she told me she was taking me to meet the God. I resisted, but she smiled saying: 'You already know me – now I want you to know him,' and, taking my hand, she guided me to a grove of oak trees. There in the middle of the grove was a beautifully antlered man-beast. The Goddess took me to him and then quietly slipped away. Suddenly, all the fears I'd had fell away – because I realised that I already knew this God. He was Herne the Hunter, Robin Hood, King Arthur, Pan and even Mr Tumnus! I realised in that dream that I had known the God all my life and that he was, in fact, all my childhood heroes rolled into one.

The gods make themselves known to us in very mysterious ways, but since having that dream I've never been afraid to invoke the witches' God. I mention this experience to let you know that you will find your own way to the particular deities that connect with you, and you will do this in your own time. If you are coming to Wicca from one of the more orthodox religions, then this may take a little longer. But in the end, all gods are one god, whatever name we call them. They are all a part of the one divinity.

Throughout this book, we will be working with specific deities that are associated with particular sabbats. Therefore it is important that you understand the basics of what the Goddess and God symbolise within witchcraft, as together they form a fundamental key to witches' principles of belief.

Ethics of the Craft

Witches believe that everyone has the right to find their own way to divinity and spirituality. You will not find a witch telling a Christian or a Muslim that their way is 'wrong', that Wicca is the only way and the Goddess the only real source of divinity. Instead, witches work towards peace and understanding between all religions, and tolerance of other people's beliefs. In addition to tolerance and understanding, there are a few other simple rules witches live by.

The first and probably the most important rule is known as the Wiccan Rede. Although the Rede in its entirety is made up of no less than 26 couplets, the final verse is the one most often quoted. It goes like this:

Eight words the Wiccan Rede fulfil,
An' it harm none, do what ye will.

The key words here are 'harm none'. That is the law we live by, and it refers to yourself and the animal kingdom too. All our spells are cast with harm to none, and contrary to popular belief, true witches do not put spells on other people. We cast spells around ourselves in order to draw in our desires. The only exception to this rule is when a witch has permission to perform a healing ritual for someone, or when she sends out love to someone or something in need.

The second rule of witchcraft illustrates why we work very hard to harm none in our spell-casting. It is known as the Threefold Law and basically states that whatever you send out – good or bad – will come back to you with three times the force and three times the consequences. In some belief systems this law is known as karma.

The final basic rule is that witches never use magic to gain control or power over someone else, nor do they work spells to influence someone or shape their decisions. This is called 'bending will' and is a form of dark magic. Smart witches steer well clear of any of the darker arts and cast all their spells in perfect love and perfect trust, with harm to none.

Seasonal living

Seasonal living is a vital part of witchcraft and magic. The natural world around us gives forth a tremendous power that can be harnessed and used to enhance our spell workings. As I write this book it is late spring. The May sun is shining and the world is gradually awakening to a new warmth. Bluebells flutter and dance in the breeze, and once again the birds are singing their spring song. Winter has passed and, although there is still a distinct chill to the evenings, it is clear that the wheel has turned and the warmer months and longer days are ahead. To many people this subtle change of season goes by in a blur, but to witches it is a time of joyful awakening, when Mother Nature is reborn after her long winter sleep.

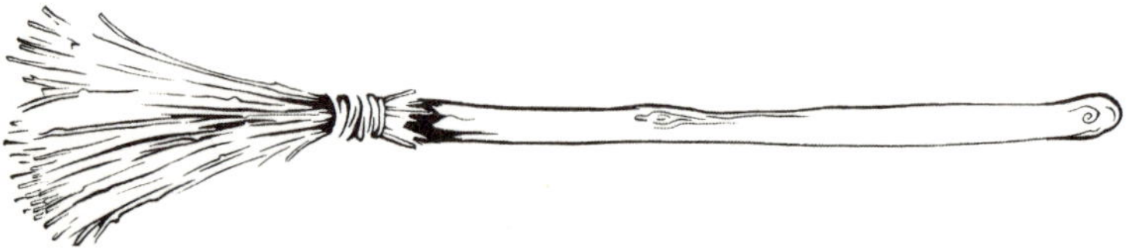

As the magical workings of this almanac are deeply rooted in nature, many using natural spell ingredients, I strongly suggest that you make a habit of getting out into nature. Spend time in your garden if you have one, walk in a local park or wood, or go for a ramble on the moors or the beach, either by yourself or with a like-minded friend. As you take these excursions, keep your eyes peeled for small natural objects that you can use in your spell-castings or as altar decorations. While you are out and about – in country or town – always observe the Countryside Code. This is simply a matter of respecting your environment:

- Use designated footpaths, where appropriate, and close all gates behind you.
- Keep dogs under proper control.
- Do not move or take away anything that is of vital importance to nature. Don't touch birds' eggs and nests, or any similar objects, even if they appear to have been abandoned.
- Do not cut anything from trees, pick flowers or dig anything up by the roots – these are the actions of vandals, not witches.

Instead, collect fallen leaves in autumn. Gather pine cones, acorns and conkers, and perhaps even bits of fallen bark from the forest floor. Curiously shaped twigs and pieces of driftwood can also be gathered without harm to nature, as can pebbles and sea shells. You can also pick up feathers, which make lovely tools and altar decorations. Enjoy your rambles and see what you can come up with.

You might also like to create a nature notebook, making a note of any wild flowers you have seen and where you saw them, perhaps with a drawing or watercolour of the plant if you are artistic. Bark and leaf rubbings can also be included, as can notes of where to find particular fungi or wild herbs. This kind of notebook may come in very useful for your magical castings. For example, if a spell calls for a sycamore leaf or a small stem of foxglove, you can flick through your nature notes and see exactly where such a plant can be found in your local area.

I have discovered that a rather novel way to collect gatherings from nature is to see what the cat dragged in – no kidding! My own cat, Pyewackett, comes into the house with dried leaves, seeds, blossoms, pods, sticky buds and bits of twig and cobwebs stuck to various parts of his anatomy. Some days he's like a walking botanical garden! If you have a cat or dog, keep a close eye on what they bring into the house. You may be able to use their 'gifts' in your magic!

The Book of Shadows

The Book of Shadows is a witch's magical diary, containing details of rituals, potions, spells, recipes, casting techniques and so on. Traditionally, it is hand-written by the witch herself and should be viewed by no one else. There are two exceptions to this rule. One is when a coven work together from one book; the other is when witchcraft is deeply rooted within a family. In this case, a family Book of Shadows may be handed down through the years with each generation adding to it. But in general, the book is created and seen only by the witch it belongs to, and is traditionally burnt at her death.

Your Book of Shadows will be as individual as you are, and no other book like it will exist. You may like to add drawings, watercolours, poems you have written and spells you have created, as well as favourite spells and rituals taken from other sources. Your nature notebook could also become a part of your Book of Shadows.

To begin with, though, you will need to obtain your Book of Shadows. These can be bought from most occult stores. They range from small leather-bound books to extraordinarily large tomes with hard, metal-hinged covers, a book lock and magical artwork embossed on the covers – a book of this description will set you back a considerable sum!

While a large, ornate Book of Shadows may be something to acquire as you move deeper into the Craft, for now a hardcover A4 book of blank pages will do fine, and is much easier on the bank balance. The important thing to remember is that your book will grow as you grow; as your knowledge of witchcraft deepens and increases, it will gradually become full and will serve as a testimony to your personal journey on the magical path.

Your magical name

Most witches choose a magical name for themselves. It helps us to connect with our inner magical selves and leave the ordinary world behind for a while. Some witches keep their magical name to themselves and treat it as a secret, while others don't. I have three magical names, two of which are secret and known only to the magical world and to myself. My third magical name is Morgana, and I often use this name in my writing and when signing Craft letters to friends.

You could choose the name of a goddess as your magical name – Diana, Branwen, Epona or Gaia, for example. Or you might decide to look to nature and choose something like Springtime, Rainbow, or the name of a tree or flower. Let your imagination lead you to something that resonates with your magical being. This is a name that you choose for yourself, so make it special and magical.

The Fundamentals of Magic

As you travel further on your magical journey, you will probably find that there is far more to spell-casting than you originally thought. Casting an effective spell requires so much more than muttering a few words and hoping for the best. The witch must remain totally focused on the positive outcome of the spell and must visualise the magical goal as if it has already occurred. She must also take into account which tools, moon phases, correspondences and so on are appropriate to the particular spell being cast. In this chapter, I'm going to tell you more about all these aspects of spell-casting.

Magical tools

In the beginning it's wise to make your tools or adapt them from household items. There are two reasons for this. Firstly, genuine ritual tools are expensive and may be beyond the pocket of someone just starting out. Secondly, not all people who set out on the magical path actually stay with it, so it's better to be absolutely certain that witchcraft is for you before you pull out your wallet! Even if you do remain a witch, it's worth remembering that as you develop your Craft skills, you will probably go through a variety of magical phases. I have found over the course of my magical life that the tools I began with are not the ones that I use now.

Once you have practised witchcraft for a few years, you might decide to invest in your beliefs and begin obtaining a set of custom-made magical tools. Once again, you will have to be smart and decide which type of tools you require. There are many out there, from gothic and traditional to those styled with a particular type of magic in mind, such as dragon, angel and Arthurian/Avalonian, to name just a few.

Because of the expense of such items, it will probably take you a while to put together a full set of magical tools, so don't worry if you have a beautiful chalice and a home-made pentacle on the same altar. The witch is the magic, not the tools she uses. Also, in buying your first formal ritual tool, you are sending out the message to the universal energies that you are ready to be fully dedicated to your magic – and the universe will respond by putting other beautiful tools in your path at a time when you can afford them. I know from experience that this is true.

The pentacle

Probably a witch's most powerful tool, the pentacle is a flat disk with the five-pointed star, or pentagram, engraved upon it. This tool is indispensable, as it is used to empower herbs and charge other correspondences that may be used in magic. It can be used to protect a space and is associated with the element Earth.

The pentacle was the first tool I made and, later on, one of the first formal tools I bought. It is traditional that the pentacle is made from a natural material such as wood, stone, slate or clay, and it should be propped upright on your altar when not in use. You can easily make a pentacle at home using cardboard or modelling clay – either the sort that doesn't need firing or the type that can be fired in an ordinary kitchen oven. Alternatively, pentacles can be bought from most occult stores, by mail order or via the internet.

The broomstick

Perhaps the most famous of magical tools, brooms – or besoms as they are also known – are used in ritual to sweep away any negative energy in the Circle, the protected space in which a witch works her magic (see page 34). It can be used purely as an altar decoration, or it can be laid on the floor to create a 'doorway' to the circle. It is also useful in workings of any magic related to faeries.

Perhaps the most magical, and certainly the most romantic use of the broomstick, is during handfastings – a witch's wedding ceremony – when the newly pledged couple jump over the broom stave to proclaim their move to a new phase of life. You can buy broomsticks from most garden centres and hardware shops, and you can easily decorate them with runic carvings or your magical name.

The chalice

The chalice is used to hold wine or juice during ritual, and any potion that is meant for ingestion should be sipped from the magical chalice. Chalices are often presented as gifts at handfastings and initiation rites, and in this sense they are called blessing cups. In rituals of witchcraft, the athame, or ritual knife, is lowered into the chalice to symbolise the divine union of male and female, God and Goddess. The chalice itself represents the element of Water.

When it comes to buying a chalice you will be spoilt for choice! Not only are there beautiful stemmed vessels in glassware and pottery stores, but the occult market is literally full of chalices, from plain ones depicting a standard pentagram to ones built on a dragon base and others that are beautifully inscribed with the face of the Green Man and inlaid with jewels. I have even seen a chalice inspired by tales of the Holy Grail – its incredible beauty was reflected in the price! With so many chalices and goblets available, you may even decide to collect them, as I do. I have a wonderful collection of pewter chalices that are all fashioned to look like characters from *The Lord of the Rings*. Among them are Gandalf, Galadriel, Celeborn and Legolas. With such a lovely range at my disposal, I always have an appropriate chalice to work with, and my altar is ever changing. Shop around and you will eventually find a chalice that speaks to you of magic and will be perfect for your personal altar.

The athame

The athame (pronounced a-thigh-me) is a ritual knife. It is used only to direct power and to carve runes and such like on to candles, wands, staffs and so on. It is never used to cut anything, so the witch usually dulls or blunts the blade. Most traditional athames have black handles and double-edged blades, but other types of athame are available too. In a magical sense the athame is used to represent Fire.

For a very long time I refused to own an athame. The reason for this was that all the ones I'd seen had a very murderous look to them! While I realised that this was an over-reaction on my part, I still couldn't bring myself to buy a ritual tool that looked so much like a weapon of violence, even if it would never be used as such.

It is only recently that I have found a blade I am happy to use in magic. I came across it in Scotland. It is actually a dirk-style paper knife that is fashioned to look like a small sword. I am very comfortable using this, as I have a passion for Arthurian legend, and a sword-like athame seems to suit me. It is worth noting that some witches, particularly those of the Celtic tradition, do use a sword instead of an athame, and you should be aware that this avenue is open to you. If a real sword is beyond your finances, you can substitute something similar. I recently bought a lovely wooden one in Sherwood Forest, and it was very inexpensive. It makes a great tool for casting a Circle especially if, like me, you're into Celtic magic.

The wand

The wand represents the element of Air. A fallen twig that reaches from the tip of your middle finger to your inner elbow – the traditional length for a wand – would be perfect. Wands can also be bought from occult stores and come in a variety of styles – carved with runes, crystal-tipped, fir-cone-tipped, strung with beads and feathers, or simply plain and unadorned. You can also buy quartz-crystal wands that are clear and pointed at one end and cloudy and round at the other. Whatever type of wand you choose, this is the one tool that you will probably be working with for a very long time, as witches do seem to get very attached to their wands.

The cauldron

The cauldron represents the Goddess and is a tool of transformation. Your cauldron should be dark in colour and should be able to withstand heat. You could use a sturdy cooking pot or casserole dish, or you might prefer to buy a traditional witches' cauldron from an occult store. These come in a wide range of sizes, so you should be able to find one to suit your budget. Cauldrons are used in magic for mixing things, and for burning fire spells and candles safely.

Other tools

In addition to the standard magical tools listed above, witches also use things like incense burners, oil burners, crystal balls, mortar and pestle, bells and chimes, mirrors, tools of divination such as pendulums and tarot cards, and figures or statues to represent the Goddess and God.

Correspondences

When you cast a spell, it is important to use the tools, directions, colours and so on that are appropriate to – or correspond with – the purpose of the spell. Items, deities, gems and so forth that correspond in this way are known as correspondences. The seasons also have correspondences – the text below lists some of them. Part of the art of creating your own spells, lies in matching all your ingredients in this way. There is plenty of information throughout the diary to help you choose appropriately.

Correspondences for spring

Angel: Raphael
Colours: yellow, white, pale greens
Crystals: aventurine, jade, rose quartz
Direction: East
Element: Air
Elemental: sylph
Flowers: snowdrop, daffodil, crocus, narcissus
Herbs and incenses: sandalwood, dragon's blood, heather, meadowsweet, lemongrass, mint, clover, catnip, all seeds
Magical hour: dawn
Moon phase: waxing
Oils: daffodil, jasmine, heather
Trees: birch, ash, apple, hazel

Correspondences for summer

Angel: Michael
Colours: gold, mid-green, purple, lilac, pink, red, orange
Crystals: citrine, carnelian, amber
Direction: South
Element: Fire
Elemental: salamander
Flowers: rose, foxglove, lilac, bluebell, sunflower
Herbs and incenses: rose, violet, St John's wort, basil, dill, thyme, jasmine, vanilla
Magical hour: noon
Moon phase: full
Oils: rose, jasmine, violet, ylang-ylang
Trees: cedar, hawthorn, oak, willow

Correspondences for autumn

Angel: Gabriel
Colours: gold, bronze, russet, brown, blue
Crystals: tiger's eye, amethyst, geode, celestite
Direction: West
Element: Water
Elemental: undine
Flowers: chrysanthemum, fallen leaves
Herbs and incenses: sandalwood, nutmeg, cinnamon, sage, mace, oakmoss, yarrow, oat, juniper
Magical hour: dusk
Moon phase: waning
Oils: oakmoss, patchouli, vetivert, cinnamon
Trees: blackthorn, rowan, sycamore

Correspondences for winter

Angel: Uriel
Colours: dark green, deep red, silver, gold, black, grey
Crystals: clear quartz crystal, opal, snowy quartz
Direction: North
Element: Earth
Elemental: gnome
Flowers: poinsettia, Christmas rose, evergreen boughs and wreaths, all berries, pine cones
Herbs and incenses: myrrh, rosemary, bayberry, bay, clove
Magical hour: midnight
Moon phase: dark moon
Oils: frankincense, myrrh, clove, cinnamon, pine
Trees: holly, ivy, fir, pine, spruce, yew

Angels

We call upon four angels in magic – you'll find more about invoking them on page 36. They are Uriel, the angel of the North, who represents magic and dreams; Raphael, the angel of the East, bringer of light and healing; Michael, the angel of the South, who represents justice and strength; and Gabriel, the angel of the West, protector of women and children, and bringer of peace.

Magical colours

As well as the seasons, colours relate to specific aspects of magic. You can use these relationships to strengthen your spell-casting.

- **Black:** strong banishings, bindings, limitations, loss, confusion, defining boundaries
- **Blue:** healing, wisdom, knowledge, dreams
- **Brown:** neutrality, stability, strength, grace, decision-making, pets, family
- **Gold:** masculinity, sun power, daylight hours, riches, the God
- **Green:** finances, security, employment, career, fertility, luck
- **Grey:** cancellations, anger, greed, envy
- **Light blue:** calmness, tranquillity, patience, understanding, good health
- **Orange:** adaptability, zest for life, energy, imagination
- **Pink:** honour, friendship, virtue, morality, success, contentment, self-love, chastity
- **Purple:** power, mild banishings, ambition, inner strength, divination
- **Red:** love, valour, courage in adversity
- **Silver:** femininity, moon power, the night, the Goddess
- **White:** purity, innocence, cleansing, childhood, truth, protection
- **Yellow:** communication, creativity, attraction, examinations, tests

The elements

The four elements play a vital role in all aspects of magic and witchcraft. Each element has its own guardian spirit, known as an elemental, and both the guardians and the elements themselves are used in spell-casting. As you can see from the list of correspondences on pages 23–4, each element is also associated with a particular season.

Earth

Powers of Earth are called upon for all aspects of fertility and growth, prosperity, luck, career and hearth magic. You can use this element to pull things towards you, so spells of acquisition should include Earth correspondences. Attuning with Earth and its guardian elementals, the gnomes, is as easy as walking in a wood, park or garden.

Air

Energies of Air are used in spells for creativity, inspiration, intellect, examination success, cultivating a particular talent, ambition and realising your dreams. The elementals of Air are the sylphs, faerie-like creatures who help govern the winds. To attune with Air, hang wind chimes around your home and garden, take a walk on a windy day or collect naturally shed feathers. You could also practise the skill of augury, which is a form of divination based on studying and interpreting the flight of birds.

Fire

Fire energies are fabulous for purging something from your life. This is a powerful element and care should be taken when invoking it and its elemental, the salamander. Always state the wish to harm none during a Fire spell. To attune with the element of Fire, light a few candles, have a barbecue or a bonfire, gaze at the flames of a real coal or log fire, or sunbathe.

Water

Water magic is used for health, healing, emotions, harmony, tranquillity and, of course, cleansings. The elementals of Water are called undines, and are mermaid-like beings that help to govern the tides and try to cleanse the pollution from our waters. Attuning with water is simple and fun – swim, take a bath or shower, enjoy a paddle in a stream or in the sea. If you feel a strong affinity with this element, then place a water feature in your home. There are some truly beautiful ones available and they need not cost a fortune. I have two. One is a beautiful leaf-shaped bowl, filled with little glass leaves which the water plays over, sounding much like a pebble-filled stream. The other is a mermaid and dolphin swimming over a rock pool. The water flows from the dolphin's mouth, down into the pool below and makes a very relaxing background sound. Water features are an excellent way to bring the magic of this element into your daily life, and as there are so many different kinds, you are sure to find one that suits you and your home.

Timing and the phases of the moon

Because magic flows in harmony with the natural world around us, the timing of spells is an integral part of Craft work. Although emergency spells should be cast as and when needed, regardless of the moon phase, other spell workings benefit from being cast at a specific time, as this helps to harness the natural power of universal energies.

The most important aspect of timing to be taken into consideration by the practitioner is the lunar cycle.

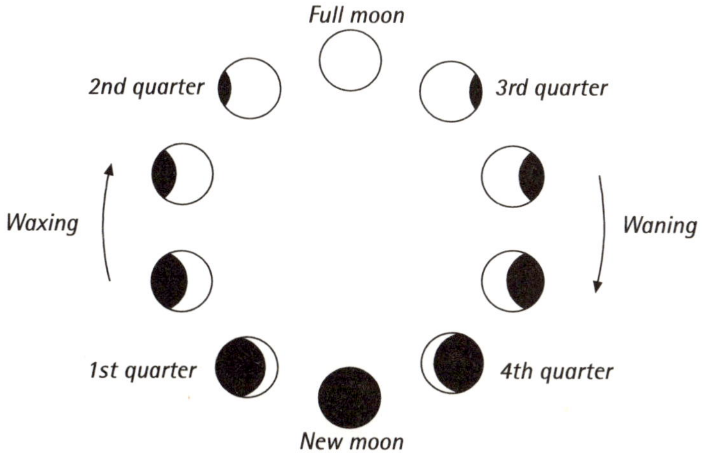

The phases of the moon

New moon ●

This is when the moon first appears, as a thin sliver of light in the sky. All spells for new ventures, new projects and new beginnings should be cast during this phase. The new moon is also good for spells concerning innocence and childhood, and for general cleansings.

Waxing moon ◐

This is the time during which the moon grows from new to full. The light gradually increases, appearing to spread from right to left. All spells that work to bring something into your life should be performed during this phase. It is particularly good for spells of growth and fertility.

Full moon ○

This phase, when all of the moon is visible, is the most powerful, and all spells can be cast effectively during it. You should also be aware that the night before and the night after the full moon are considered just as potent, effectively giving three whole nights of full moon power.

Waning moon ◑

This is the time when the moon grows smaller in the sky, appearing to shrink from right to left. Witches use this phase to cast spells that remove unhelpful influences from their lives. These influences may range from poverty and bad habits to bad relationships and negative people. If you want to gently rid your life of something, then use the waning moon phase.

Dark moon

The moon is said to be dark when it isn't visible in the sky. This is traditionally a time of rest, and the only magic worked during this phase is banishings (which pull something or someone away from you) and bindings (which freeze someone's or something's power and influence over you).

Blue moon

A blue moon occurs when there is more than one full moon in a single calendar month. This only happens once every few years, hence the expression 'once in a blue moon'. This is a time for setting long-term goals and casting spells to help manifest your dreams. Blue moon energy is rare and should never be wasted – you should always cast some kind of goal-setting magic on this night. There are no blue moons in 2006. The last one was on 31 July 2004 and the next will be on 30 June 2007 at 13.48.

Moon signs through the zodiac

The sign of the zodiac in which the moon appears is also relevant to your magic. This changes about every two and a half days and lends a different character to your spells.

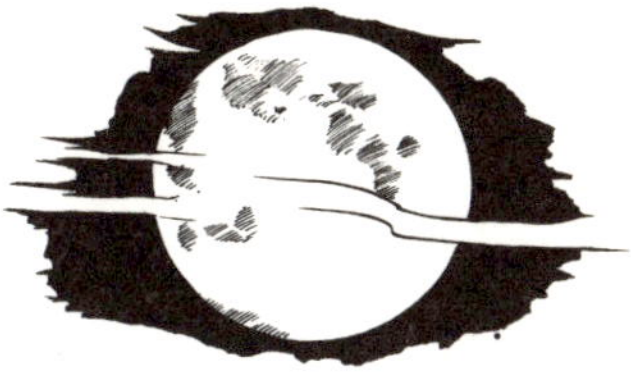

♈ **Moon in Aries:** a good time for new beginnings but carries the danger of being too impulsive.

♉ **Moon in Taurus:** a more cautious and practical influence, ideal for long-lasting results, but be careful to avoid inflexibility.

♊ **Moon in Gemini:** a versatile moon, good for fun and communication but with a tendency to fickleness.

♋ **Moon in Cancer:** an emotional and nurturing influence; your feelings may be particularly sensitive.

♌ **Moon in Leo:** full of generosity and ambition – an influence for getting ahead and putting yourself first.

♍ **Moon in Virgo:** practical and efficient, a good time for organisation and attention to detail as well as issues relating to health.

♎ **Moon in Libra:** a sociable time with a strong sense of balance.

♏ **Moon in Scorpio:** a passionate and resourceful time, but one in which to avoid confrontation.

♐ **Moon in Sagittarius:** spontaneity and exploration are the keys to this influence, with a degree of restlessness.

♑ **Moon in Capricorn:** ambition, hard work and a serious view of life are the features of this lunar influence; be careful not to ignore the needs of others.

♒ **Moon in Aquarius:** an unconventional moon, bringing change and individuality.

♓ **Moon in Pisces:** emotional sensitivity and spirituality are relevant under this influence, with a tendency to fragility.

Days of power

Each day of the week also lends different energies to your work.

☽ **Monday:** the day of the moon. Good for spells that relate to your home, pets, family, feminine issues, psychic development and dreams.

♂ **Tuesday:** Mars rules this day, making it perfect for any positive confrontation. Magic for business, work, getting your point across, courage and bravery should be worked on this day.

☿ **Wednesday:** ruled by Mercury, the winged messenger, so all spells for communication and creativity should be cast on this day.

♃ **Thursday:** ruled by Jupiter, this is a day for money and prosperity spells, as well as holiday and travel magic.

♀ **Friday:** this day belongs to Venus, so all spells for love, friends and socialising will be enhanced if performed on this day.

♄ **Saturday:** ruled by Saturn, this is a good day to do magical work around paying off debts or to magically call in money owed to you. It's also good for releasing negative thought patterns and overcoming bad habits.

☉ **Sunday:** the day of the sun. This is a great day for magic of self-love and masculine issues. It's fabulous for 'me time'.

The witch's altar

The Wiccan altar is the power centre of the witch's magic. It is here that the witch keeps her magical tools and performs spell-castings, rituals and the seasonal rites of the sabbats. While there are some magical practitioners out there who have dedicated a whole room to their magical interests (traditionally known as an altar room), most of us simply don't have the luxury of that much space and have instead set aside a corner (or several corners) of a room somewhere. My own altar room is my bedroom, and I've painted this room a deep violet – the colour of magic, meditation and psychic dreams.

Altars are as individual as people are, and if you are in contact with other Wiccans you will probably have noticed that their altars will look very different from yours and from each other. You will also find that your altar goes through a number of changes. Just like your Book of Shadows, it will develop, growing as you grow, and you will add and take things away from your magical set-up. Over the years I have created altars dedicated to the angels, dragons, the Goddess, the God and to nature itself. Quite a few surfaces in my home have been turned into altars at some time or other, from the mantelpiece (which still serves as a dragon altar) to coffee tables, bookcases and my dressing table, which was in use as a working altar for a long time. I recently decided to buy a new altar table to set up in a private corner of the bedroom. All I knew was that I wanted my new altar table to be round, and I was fortunate enough to come across a beautiful pewter mermaid with a round glass table-top balanced on her upraised arms. It's perfect for witchcraft and looks great with all my Craft tools on it.

Your altar surface should be one that suits you and your home. Pretty much anything goes, as long as the surface you choose is sturdy and has space for your tools and so on. It should be placed in a room that is private, so a bedroom or study is ideal. Traditionally, only candlelight is used to light the altar, so two white candles should be placed towards the back of your altar. These are called illuminator candles. Between these two candles place a representation of your chosen divinity. I use a large white marble figure of Aphrodite, the goddess of love and beauty, which was a gift from my mother – beautiful gifts always have a place on a magical altar.

In addition, my altar holds a pentacle, an athame, a crystal ball held up by three pewter dragons, a small jar of sea salt, rose quartz and amethyst crystals, an incense holder shaped like a wizard and a pewter goblet in the form of Legolas, the elf from *The Lord of the Rings*. It's an eclectic mixture, including all the things I love about magic.

However, you might decide to follow a specific theme – faeries for instance, or the pentagram. Perhaps your altar will represent the God and will be full of stags and green men. Alternatively, you might create a natural altar, using flowers and leaves, or you might choose to make an altar of the sea, full of shells, driftwood and so on. Throughout this book, we will be looking at many different types of altar set-up, but don't feel that you have to adopt one of them; use your imagination, be resourceful and create your altar to reflect your personality and your own ideas of magic.

Practical Magic

So far we have dealt with the theory of witchcraft. In this chapter we will look at the practical side of spell-casting.

Perhaps the most important part of any spell or ritual is the intent and focus the practitioner brings to it. Many people fail in their first attempts at spell-casting simply because they were not focused enough, their mind was elsewhere or the clarity of their magical intent was hazy. For magic to succeed and spells to be effective, it is vital that you strongly visualise the intended outcome of the spell and that you remain entirely focused on this visualisation throughout the ritual.

Those new to magic may find this aspect of spell work difficult at first, but the key to success is practice. The more you practise, the better you will get and the easier spell-castings will become. Remember that visualisation is something you do naturally anyway; you simply need to learn to become more aware of it and apply it to your magic. If you would like to learn more about this technique, have a look at my book *Candleburning Rituals,* where visualisation is explained for those new to magic.

Casting a Circle

Witches work their magic within a protected space known as the Circle. Here rituals are performed, spells are cast and meditations or prayers are offered. The Circle is a temporary space. It is created by the magical practitioner before she does her work, and it is carefully taken down afterwards.

The Circle is a secure boundary that keeps all negative energies away from you and your magic. It also contains the magical power raised within its 'walls' until the practitioner is ready to release it. There are probably as many different types of Circle-casting as there are witches. Some Circles are seen as electric blue light, others are made up of imaginary falling leaves, snowflakes, hedgerows and so on. Although known as a Circle, this protective space is actually a sphere that completely encompasses the witch and her work.

Two terms that you will come across in Circle-casting and in other spell-casting practices are deosil and widdershins. Deosil is the Wiccan term for clockwise, and widdershins is anti-clockwise. You always go deosil to cast and widdershins to uncast.

Below is a basic Circle-casting. Feel free to experiment and use your imagination to cast different forms of Circle. Remember, though, that the Circle should always be cast before any sort of spell work is performed, and your altar should be contained within it, either to the north or to the east.

A basic Circle-casting

- Stand with your arm outstretched and, pointing with your wand or athame, walk around (or turn if the space is small) in a circle three times in a deosil direction.
- Imagine that a stream of blue light forms a circle around you.
- Now raise your arms and imagine that the light expands both upwards and below you, thus creating the magical sphere. Clap once and say:

  This Circle is sealed!

- You are now ready to work your chosen spell. After casting your spell, you will need to take down the magic Circle. The following section tells you how to do this.

Taking down the Circle

- Walk the Circle three times in a widdershins direction, visualising the light being drawn back into your wand or athame.
- Now clap once and say:

This Circle is open, but never broken.

This effectively means that you have released the power of the Circle, not destroyed it.

If you have a besom, or broom, you might like to carefully sweep the magical area clean before casting your circle. This is done by calmly sweeping the air a few inches above the floor, and will remove any negative energy that may be lingering around.

Calling the quarters

Once the Circle has been cast, the witch may call on particular guardians either to protect the space or to assist with the ritual – this is most often the case for sabbatic rituals and workings of strong magic. Calling in the guardians is known as 'calling the quarters', and there are many different types of guardian that can be called.

When you are calling the quarters, it is especially important that you are clear about what you are visualising, as depending on the job you want your guardians to do, you will visualise them in a particular way. For instance, if you want the guardians to protect the circle, you should visualise them facing outwards, away from you and the Circle. In this way they are ready to deflect any negative energies that may be heading towards your Circle and will thus make the sacred space stronger. If you want your chosen guardians to assist you with the spell, however, you should visualise them facing inwards, towards you.

When witches say 'assist', we mean, of course, that the guardians will lend their magical energies to the spell-working – they won't go around lighting the candles for you and smudging the area with sage! They will simply act as a power boost for the magical practitioner.

Be aware that when you are invoking the guardians, you are calling on very real energies. Just because these powerful entities can only be seen in your mind's eye, does not make them any less real, and, metaphorically speaking, they can and will slap your wrists if you're rude to them! Be warned and proceed with due respect.

Below are some of my favourite quarter calls. These are the ones I use most often and feel entirely comfortable with. Use whichever ones appeal to you but please don't invoke any guardian you feel uncomfortable with. If dragons scare you, don't use them – work with something smaller! The four archangels are excellent quarter guardians, both for the neophyte and the adept witch.

Calling the angels

- Stand within your Circle and face north. Raise both arms high above your head and, visualising Uriel facing outwards from the Circle, begin the call:

I call on Uriel, angel of the North,
Angel of magic and dreams, protector of witches.
I call you here to guard and protect this sacred space.

- Now face east and, visualising Raphael facing outwards from the Circle, say:

I call on Raphael, angel of the East,
Light bearer and divine healer.
I call you here to guard and protect this sacred space.

- Now face south and, visualising Michael facing outwards from the Circle, say:

I call on Michael, angel of the South,
Angel of justice, valour and strength,
I call you here to guard and protect this sacred space.

- Finally, face west and, visualising Gabriel facing outwards from the Circle, say:

I call on Gabriel, angel of the West,
Protector of women and children, bringing peace to all.
I call you here to guard and protect this sacred space.

I generally enhance these calls by placing candles and figures of angels at each of the four quarters.

Calling the elementals

- Stand within your circle and face north. Raise both arms high above your head and, visualising the gnomes facing outwards from the Circle, begin the call:

Hail to the elementals of the North!
I call on the gnomes, spirits of Earth,
Powers of growth and abundance.
I call you here to guard and protect my sacred space.

- Face east and, visualising the sylphs facing outwards from the Circle, say:

Hail to the elementals of the East!
I call on the sylphs, spirits of Air,
Powers of wisdom and truth.
I call you here to guard and protect my sacred space.

- Face the south and, visualising the salamanders facing outwards from the Circle, say:

Hail to the elementals of the South!
I call on the salamanders, spirits of Fire,
Powers of passion and love.
I call you here to guard and protect my sacred space.

- Face the West and, visualising the undines facing outwards from the Circle, say:

Hail to the elementals of the West!
I call on the undines, spirits of Water,
Powers of healing and prophecy.
I call you here to guard and protect my sacred space.

You can enhance these calls by placing candles and figures at the appropriate quarters, such as a gnome at North, a fairy at East, a dragon or lizard at South or a mermaid at West.

A word about dragons

When it comes to dragons, there is a special set of rules, the most important being, they are bigger than we are, so be nice! It is particularly important to invoke dragon power respectfully. Never 'summon' a dragon as they can be quite testy creatures – call to him politely!

I suggest you make yourself known to the dragons before performing the following quarter call. You could do this by working with them during meditations, or by reading about them. You could also buy a picture or poster of a dragon to adorn your ritual space, or even create a small altar dedicated to the realm of dragons, which is most flattering to these fabulous creatures! I started a dragon altar many years ago, by placing one or two dragon figures on my mantelpiece and burning incense there regularly. This altar has grown over time and now includes dragon-shaped candle holders, incense burners, chalices and lots of dragon statues! It is one of my favourite spaces within my home, and I highly recommend creating such a dragon altar to anyone who wishes to work magically with these majestic and powerful creatures.

The following call can be enhanced by placing dragon statues and the appropriately coloured candle at each quarter.

Calling the dragons

- Stand within your Circle and face north. Raise both arms high above your head and, visualising the green dragon facing outwards from the Circle, begin the call:

I call on the green dragon of Earth,
He of the leaf-like scales,
He of the greenwood glen.
Powers of fertility and stability,
I invite you here to guard and protect my sacred space.
Hail Draconis!

- Face east and, visualising the golden dragon facing outwards from the Circle, say:

I call on the golden dragon of Air,
He of the sunlight rays,
He of the roaring wind.
Powers of creativity and communication,
I invite you here to guard and protect my sacred space.
Hail Draconis!

- Face south and, visualising the red dragon facing outwards from the Circle, say:

I call on the red dragon of Fire,
He of the fiery glow,
He of the smouldering embers deep.
Powers of cleansing and courage,
I invite you here to guard and protect my sacred space.
Hail Draconis!

- Face west and, visualising the blue dragon facing outwards from the Circle, say:

I call on the blue dragon of Water,
He of the liquid grace,
He of the shimmering sea.
Powers of inspiration and intuition,
I invite you here to guard and protect my sacred space.
Hail Draconis!

During all your quarter calls remember to visualise clearly. In all these examples, we have asked the guardians to protect our space, but all these calls can be altered by removing the line about protection and instead saying: 'I call you here and ask for your assistance in my magical working'. You would also visualise the guardians facing inwards, towards the circle and yourself.

Releasing the quarters

Once you have completed your ritual, you must release all the guardians before taking down the circle. Do this by moving around the circle and releasing the quarters in reverse order (beginning in the west and moving back to finish at the north).

- At each quarter, raise your arms and say:

I give thanks for your presence within this sacred space.
I acknowledge and thank you for your protection/assistance. I now release you from that duty, in the name of the Lady and the Lord. Hail and farewell! Blessed Be!

Blow or snuff out the candle, and move on to the next quarter. All quarters must be released after working magic, and you might like to smudge the area with incense too, which will help to disperse any energies left over from the ritual.

Grounding

This is the final step of any magical endeavour. After releasing the quarters and taking down the circle, it is important that you release any magical energy that is lingering around you, as it can leave you feeling fey and slightly 'spaced out'. This is known as 'grounding' the energy, and the simplest way to do it is to lie down on the floor for a few minutes, allowing the energy to drain away. Afterwards, eat and drink something to re-balance your own inner energies and do something quiet and peaceful for at least an hour or two, before going about your normal day.

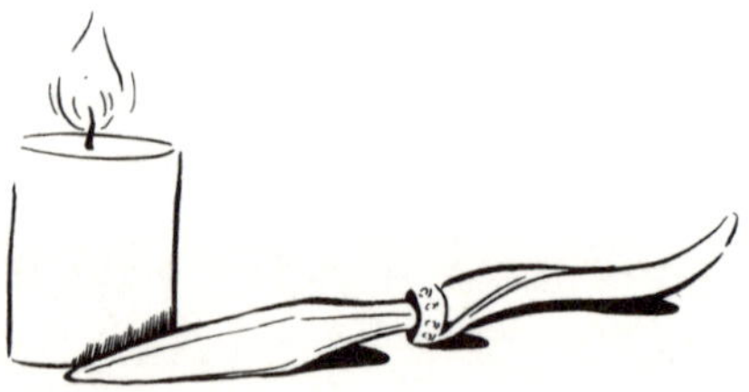

Triple Goddess moon altar

As we have already noted, the moon plays an integral part in the Craft, so it stands to reason that witches should perform rituals at particular moon phases in honour of the Triple Goddess. Special rites are performed at full moon and new moon; and at the time of the dark moon, when no magic is worked, the Crone is honoured and acknowledged in some way.

A good way to keep in touch with moon energy is to set up a Triple Goddess altar. This could be a part of your main altar, or it could be an entirely different set-up. Moon altars are some of the most beautiful Wiccan altars around, and there are many images of the Goddess to choose from to adorn such a space.

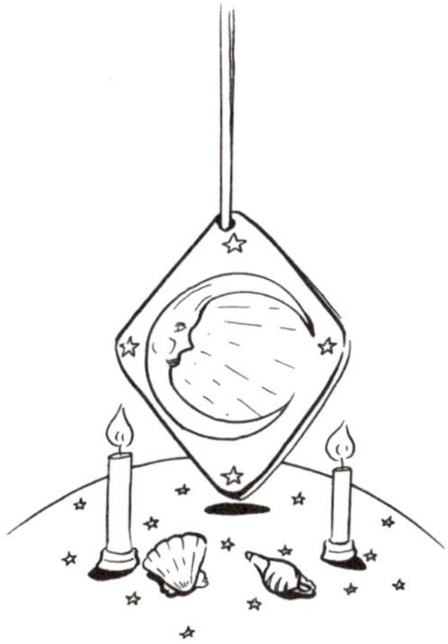

To create a Triple Goddess altar you will need two white or silver candles as illuminators. These should be set in sturdy silver or pewter candlesticks. Your altar surface should preferably be round and covered with a white or silver altar cloth. However, if the table-top is made of glass, an altar cloth is unnecessary as the round piece of glass in itself makes a nice representation of the moon. Next, think about the space around the altar and add appropriate decorations. Some ideas you might try are crescent moon wall plaques, crescent moon wind chimes and pictures or posters depicting either a moon goddess or the lunar cycle. A silver mirror ball, or perhaps a sphere of faceted crystal, hung to represent the full moon is also appropriate, as is a large round wall mirror.

Turning to the altar itself, you should include a chalice that depicts the emblem of the Triple Goddess – three crescent moons – (these can be bought from occult shops) or perhaps the Galadriel goblet from the *Lord of the Rings* range. In addition, and perhaps most importantly, this type of altar should hold representations of each of the three aspects of the Goddess – that is Maiden, Mother and Crone. My own altar holds figures of Diana as Maiden, Aphrodite as Mother, and the Crone wearing a purple hooded robe, which hides her face and adds to her mystery! I change each of these figures around in accordance with the moon phase so that at any given stage in the lunar cycle, the appropriate goddess figure is stood between the two candles, with her sister goddesses in the background. In addition, my altar holds a crescent moon incense burner and a moon crown.

Choose items for your Triple Goddess altar that are appealing to you and deities that strike a chord in your heart. Add pearls, opals, moonstones, snowy quartz and clear quartz crystals and your moon altar will be a power centre that will bring the magic and light of the Goddess into your home.

Spells for special days

The following spells are designed to be performed at your discretion throughout the year. Here you will find magical ways to celebrate marriages, birthdays, new babies and so on, as well as traditional rituals for the full and new moon, which should be performed monthly at the appropriate time. Happy casting!

Esbats

Esbats are the rituals performed to honour the phases of the moon. Usually witches perform a brief rite of welcoming at the new moon and a larger ritual at the time of the full moon. These rituals are performed every month, unless for some reason you have other commitments, such as work or nursing a sick family member. Even if a full ritual is out of the question, however, you can at least light the candles and incense on your Triple Goddess altar and offer up a prayer or meditation in acknowledgement of the lunar phase.

New moon esbat

If your garden is private, you could set up an outdoor altar and perform this ritual outside beneath the new moon. As we have said, the new moon is the time of the Maiden, so the Maiden Goddess figure should be in the central position on your moon altar. If you haven't yet acquired your goddess figures, then appropriate pictures, postcards or tarot cards can be used instead.

Purpose of ritual: to honour the new moon

What you need: sandalwood incense, white wine or grape juice, a croissant and your favourite filling, a sheet of paper, a pencil

- Light the illuminator candles and sit for a moment thinking of all that the Maiden represents. She is the symbol of new life, joy, anticipation, childhood, innocence, pure ideals and virginity. Light the incense and say:

  I light this incense in acknowledgement of the new moon. In this the time of the Maiden, help me to find joy in all things and to sow the seeds of my dreams.

- Now take the paper and write upon it one goal that you would like to work towards. This could be a new job, a house move, or whatever is appropriate at this time in your life. Sit for a while and concentrate on this goal, asking the Maiden to help you achieve it, and then fold the spell paper in half and place it beneath your Maiden statue.
- Now chant the following incantation:

  In this right and ready hour,
I call upon the ancient power.
I welcome the Maiden's shimmering glow.
As I will, it shall be so.

- Afterwards you might like to meditate for a while or commune with the Goddess through a visualisation.
- Finally, drink the wine and eat the croissant (the crescent shape represents the new moon). This post-ritual feast is traditionally known as cakes and ale. Be sure to save a little of each as an offering to the natural world, leaving them in your garden.
- Blow out the candles and return to your evening activities.

Full moon esbat

The night of the full moon is the most powerful time for working magic. Because of this, a full moon esbat will normally include spell workings and divinations. This is also a great time for magical wish-making and for giving thanks for all that you enjoy in your life.

Once again your full moon ritual can be worked outside if you have a private outdoor space. If you like, you can travel to a secluded spot to work the ritual, but, of course, you must use your common sense and think of safety first.

If you are working the ritual indoors, try to perform it where you have a view of the moon. Reflecting the full moon through a mirror, or cauldron of water is very magical, so you might like to try this.

Purpose of ritual: to embrace the power of the full moon

What you need: your athame or wand, Night Queen incense, white wine or grape juice, a scone and butter

- Make sure that the Mother Goddess figure is in the central position on your moon altar and the illuminator candles are lit. Now sit for a time and think of all that the Mother Goddess represents. She is abundance and prosperity, fruitfulness and great joy. She is nurturing and the Mother of All, and will offer her protection to those who ask.

- Now light the Night Queen incense and work any magical spells you have planned.

- Once your spells have been cast, it's time to perform the most traditional part of the full moon ritual, drawing down the moon – or pulling the magnetic power of the moon into yourself. Stand with a clear view of the full moon, and with your feet apart and your athame or wand in your right hand, raise both arms above your head.

- Point the athame or wand towards the moon and concentrate on pulling down its power, drawing it into the tip of your wand or athame blade. As you do so, say these words:

I am a Priestess/Priest of the Goddess;
I walk the old ways.
I am a weaver of magic and light.
I now draw down the power of the moon;

I take into myself, the magic of the Great Mother,
The gift of the Goddess. Blessed be!

- Now point the athame at your heart and visualise the power being transferred from the blade into your body. Feel the magic surge through you, and then sit before your moon altar in meditation or communion with your chosen goddess.
- During this esbat, it is also traditional to recite The Charge of the Goddess, a poem by Doreen Valiente, one of the most influential high priestesses in formal magical tradition. This can be bought as a poster or wall hanging from most occult shops.
- End your ritual by eating the scone (round to represent the full moon) and drinking the wine or juice. Remember to save a little of each to empty into the garden as an offering. Put out your candles and clear away your ritual things.

Dark moon esbat

No magic is worked at this time, but the Crone figure should be placed in the middle of your moon altar, and the candles can be lit and incense burned while you meditate and commune with this aspect of the goddess, the Dark Mother.

Handfasting rituals

A handfasting, as I mentioned before, is a witch's wedding ceremony. Some witches have a handfasting in addition to a traditional wedding, while for others a handfasting is the only ceremony held. It may be private, with yourself and your loved one, or it may be witnessed by family and friends in a more traditional style. There are three types of handfasting, each pledging the participants for a different length of time. The first binds them for a year and a day, and this can be renewed every 366 days if required. The second binds for 'as long as true love shall last', and the third states that the 'bond is eternal'. It is entirely a matter of personal choice how long you are pledged to each other.

The ceremony is called a handfasting because the hands of the participants are bound together using a cord that they have made themselves. This 2.75-metre/9-foot cord is made up of three ribbons of the couple's chosen colours, knotted at one end. The lovers take turns to hold and plait the ribbons together, thus creating the handfasting cord. In Scotland the cord is sometimes replaced with a length of clan tartan.

A handfasting is a ceremony created by the couple themselves. Vows are spoken and then a pledge of heart and body is given. While there are variations, a simple pledge would go something like this:

My heart to thee, my body to thee,
For a year and a day / as long as true love
shall last / our bond is eternal.
So mote it be.

The couple then drink from the same blessing cup and jump the handfasting broom. After that, their hands are unbound and the festivities begin.

Wiccaning ritual

A wiccaning is the witches' equivalent of a christening. At its simplest it is a baby naming and blessing ceremony. It can also act to place the child on the Wiccan path, although most parents prefer to wait until the child is old enough to choose his or her own belief system for this aspect of the ritual. As with most Wiccan rites of passage, a wiccaning is designed with the wishes of the individuals concerned in mind.

Witch's birthday ritual

A birthday is a fabulous time for ritual. On this day a witch gives thanks for the blessings of life and all that she enjoys. A witch's birthday ritual can be a private affair or it can take place among like-minded friends. You can hold the ritual in a sacred outdoor space or in the privacy of your own home. It is your birthday, so you choose.

Your altar should be set up with your favourite colours and flowers, maybe your birth stone and perhaps a representation of your astrological sign. Altar figures of the goddesses and gods you feel an affinity with are appropriate, as are candles of all kinds – especially birthday candles. You might also like to add a statue of your totem or power animal.

The ritual feast should be made up of all your favourite foods and drinks, and all diet plans (other than the medical variety) should be put on hold! This is your day, your ritual. It's a time for noting your achievements and setting goals for the future. Play your favourite music and treat yourself to a new ritual tool or altar decoration, something that connects your everyday life with that of your magical one. Celebrate; ask the universal powers to bring you gifts of abundance, happiness, love and health; and enjoy being you!

The Witch's Diary 2006

In the following pages, you can track the year and its magical influences and rituals, and you can use the diary pages to jot down events or experiences of the passing year. The following reference pages will provide a useful reminder of some of the information in the book and help to familiarise you with the various symbols used.

All times are given in Universal Time.

Sun signs

Sign	*Symbol*	*Ruling planet*
Aries	♈	Mars
Taurus	♉	Venus
Gemini	♊	Mercury
Cancer	♋	Moon
Leo	♌	Sun
Virgo	♍	Mercury
Libra	♎	Venus
Scorpio	♏	Pluto
Sagittarius	♐	Jupiter
Capricorn	♑	Saturn
Aquarius	♒	Uranus
Pisces	♓	Neptune

Moon phases

Phase	*Symbol*	*Suitable magic*
New moon	●	For new ventures and cleansings
Waxing moon	◐	To draw things towards you
Full moon	○	When the moon exerts the greatest power
Waning moon	◑	For meditation and study, or for magic to push away negative energies

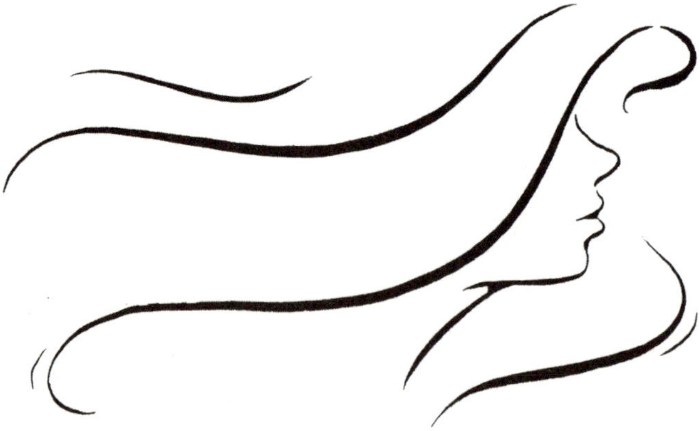

Dawn and dusk

Times are given for London, England.

Planets

Planet	*Symbol*	*Qualities*
Sun	☉	Warm, confident and generous
Mercury	☿	Opportunistic and communicative
Venus	♁	Emotional and loving
Mars	♂	Enthusiastic and energetic
Jupiter	♃	Wise and learned
Saturn	♄	Responsible and close to the heart of things
Uranus	♅	Inventive and original
Neptune	♆	Related to dreams and illusions
Moon	☽	Reflective and sensitive
Pluto	♇	Powerful

Days of the week

Day	*Ruled by*	*Planet*	*Suitable magic*
Monday	Moon	☽	Home, family and psychic development
Tuesday	Mars	♂	Business, work and confidence
Wednesday	Mercury	☿	Communication and creativity
Thursday	Jupiter	♃	Prosperity and travel
Friday	Venus	♀	Friendship, love and sociability
Saturday	Saturn	♄	Money and releasing negative emotions
Sunday	Sun	☉	Personal healing and self-esteem

Moon signs

Sign	*Symbol*	*Suitable magic*
Aries	♈	For new, ambitious projects and fast results
Taurus	♉	For more cautious and long-lasting progress
Gemini	♊	For communication and versatility
Cancer	♋	For emotional nurturing and growth
Leo	♌	For ambition, generosity and self
Virgo	♍	For organisation and efficiency
Libra	♎	For social awareness and co-operation
Scorpio	♏	For resourcefulness and passion
Sagittarius	♐	For growth and spontaneity
Capricorn	♑	For hard work and seriousness
Aquarius	♒	For change, freedom and the unconventional
Pisces	♓	For intuition and sensitivity

The Witch's God

Who am I? How do you know me?
Am I the face in the leaves of a tree?
Am I the satyr who skips through the woods?
Or Bacchus who makes the wine taste so good?
Am I Apollo who rides through the sky
Bringing the sun on its journey so high?
What is my name? Whose face do you see?
Whose name do you call as you invoke me?
Osiris, Adonis, Eros or Pan,
Robin of Sherwood or the Green Man?
Who do you call as you work through the spell?
Which aspect of me do you know so well?
Hero, protector, warrior, lord?
Bearer of arrows? Wielder of sword?
For I am the Trickster, I am the sun,
I am the Holly King when summer is gone.
I will protect you, shield you from harm,
For I am the battle, yet also the calm.
The Warrior Spirit is my gift to you,
Giving you courage, guiding you through.
I am the god with the goat-foot stance,
I am He, the Lord of the Dance.

January

The month of January is named after the Roman god, Janus. He is the god of gates and doorways and is generally represented as having a double-faced head, enabling him to look both forwards and backwards at the same time. This means that he is in perfect tune with this time of year, when we look forward to the coming months while reflecting on what the previous year has brought our way. Janus can help us to see more clearly both where we have been and where we are heading in our lives, and he teaches us that the past and the future are inextricably linked. His image is used in ancient temples and buildings as a guardian, and if you happen to find a statue or picture of Janus, you should place it in the hallway or near the door to your house, asking Janus to protect your space and those within it.

The ancient Celts linked each month of the year to a particular tree. This system was known as the Ogham and was used as a form of divination, in turn linking each tree with a letter of the alphabet and giving it a particular symbol. The Celtic tree oracle and divination sticks are still used by practitioners of Celtic magic. Trees were extremely important to the Celts, as they provided tools, shelter, weapons, medicines, dyes and even some types of food, such as nuts, fruits and berries. They were also seen as sources of great strength, wisdom and protection.

The tree the Celts associated with January was the fearn or alder. This is a water-loving tree and so can be found on river banks and near streams. To the Celts it symbolised emotional strength, stamina and spiritual protection. Because alder wood is so strong, it was often used in building foundations or to make boats. As such, it became linked to overcoming obstacles and bridging gaps between individuals or groups of people. At its essence the alder is a tree of communication and protection.

In addition to the alder tree, the narcissus flower and the herbs lavender and pine, are also associated with the month of January. In the language of flowers, the narcissus is symbolic of self-love. However, there are different aspects of self-love. While on the one hand we sometimes need to appreciate ourselves a little more, on the other hand, there are those who think too much of themselves! Do make time for yourself, but not to the detriment of loved ones around you.

To fully attune with this month, try mixing an incense made up of equal parts of lavender and pine, and burn it at your altar, which could be decorated with a vase of narcissus flowers. This will fill your sacred space with the fragrance of the season.

January

Dawn 07.59
Dusk 16.09

Sunday 1st			
Moon quarter	1st (waxing)	Special	New Year's Day
Moon sign	♑ 12.14 ♒		Horse's Birthday
Colour	Silver		(northern hemisphere)
Herb or incense	Pine		20.18 Venus ♀
Crystal	Clear Quartz		enters Capricorn ♑
Sun sign	♑		

NEW YEAR'S DAY

For many of us the new year dawns on a world covered in a blanket of snow, or at least a dull grey sky filled with the prospect of rain! The air is icy and a chill wind blows. The trees stand barren of leaves and spring seems a long way off.

The first day of the new year is a time for thinking ahead and deciding what goals should be aimed for during the next 12 months.

I find that keeping a regular diary is a wonderful way to record how far I've come on my personal path. In looking through old diaries, something I always find myself doing at this time of year, I can see that things I once regarded as pipe dreams are now a reality in my life. So I begin the new year by writing down a list of goals that I would like to achieve. I usually write this list at the back of my new diary and I generally aim for around 20 goals per year. Of course, some of these are left unrealised come December – but I do normally manage to achieve at least half of them. It's a very positive way to begin this new cycle of the seasons, and I've also found that a positive goal will have far more chance of success than a half-hearted resolution!

New Year Ritual

Purpose of ritual: to set goals for the next 12 months
What you need: a new diary, a sheet of paper, an envelope, a silver pen, a white candle, your athame or an inscribing tool, a special box

- First relax and think of all that you have accomplished so far. You might like to set up a relaxing scene by lighting candles and cosy lamps, burning sweet-smelling incense or oils and having a glass of wine to hand. I like to pile cushions on the floor and sit working this ritual at the coffee table before the fire.
- Once you are calm and comfortable, begin to make a list of goals you would like to achieve within the next 12 months. These goals should be feasible, and you should write down no less than five and no more than 20. They can relate to any area of your life. Some of my goals over the years have included gaining a publishing contract, decorating a room in my house, visiting the Scottish Highlands, and obtaining a writer's bureau and a four-poster bed. Your own list may be similar, or it may be completely different.
- Once you have drafted your list, copy it into your new diary, using the silver pen, and then fold up the original list and place it in the envelope.
- Divide the candle into as many sections as you have goals, using your athame or inscribing tool.
- Keep the envelope and the candle in a special box on your altar, and every time you achieve a goal, place a tick on your diary list, date it and allow the candle to burn down one section.
- At the end of the year, transfer any unaccomplished goals that you are still dedicated to to your new list, and keep the old list in your old diary as testimony to your achievements.

Prosperity Spell

Purpose of ritual: to bring prosperity throughout the next 12 months
What you need: 12 dried bay leaves, a gold or silver pen, an envelope, a cauldron, matches, your pentacle, your purse or wallet

- Take all the above items to your altar and cast the Circle. Place the bay leaves on the pentacle to charge.
- Now sit for a few moments and think of all the prosperity you wish to attract in the coming year. This could take the form of holidays, household appliances, clothes, books, luxury items, champagne, cash in the bank and so on.
- Next, using the gold or silver pen, write the name of a month on each bay leaf, beginning with January. Each bay leaf now represents a month of the coming year and will help to bring prosperity into your life.
- Take the leaf that represents January and put it in your purse or wallet. Put the remaining leaves in the envelope and leave it on the altar. At the end of each month, burn the old bay leaf in the cauldron, asking the spirits of fire to bring you continued prosperity, and put the next bay leaf into your purse.

HORSE'S BIRTHDAY

In the northern hemisphere January 1st is also known as the horse's birthday (in the southern hemisphere this celebration is held on 1 August). As horses have played such a major role in the history of humankind, it is fitting that a day should be held sacred to them. They have been our companions, our pets, our means of transport, our farm labourers and even our fellow soldiers in war. No other animal has given itself in service to human beings for so many centuries, and much of our cultural evolution is due to the horse, a fact that is often forgotten. These noble creatures, who are powerful yet gentle, beautiful yet humble, and strong enough to kill a man yet kind enough to take him on his back, are sadly overlooked. But today we celebrate, giving thanks and sincere admiration to these noble creatures, and calling on the goddess, Epona, who protects them.

Ritual of Epona

In Celtic mythology, Epona is the goddess of horses. So popular was she that even the Romans adopted her and set up monuments to her at the barracks of their cavalry, and she was revered all over Europe. Some believe that the great white chalk horse, carved into the hillside near Wantage in southern England, was created in honour of Epona.

There is no doubt that the Celts held their horses in high esteem. Epona was called upon to protect horses and stables, mares during foaling and youngsters first learning to ride. We still invoke her blessings today, by hanging the traditional horseshoe above the door to bring good luck and protection. As she is also a fertility goddess, she is sometimes depicted bearing sheaves of wheat, and so is yet another aspect of the Mother Goddess. In a more negative sense, she is associated with the white Night Mare, bringing terror to the darkest hours and forcing us to face our deepest fears.

Purpose of ritual: to attune with Epona, the Celtic goddess of horses
What you need: white and gold candles, ribbons and other decorations; a picture or figure of a horse (preferably a white one) or a horseshoe

- Epona's colours are white and gold, so for this ritual decorate your altar accordingly. If you have a horse of your own, or know of some grazing in your area, chop carrots lengthways and place these on your altar too. After the ritual these can be given to your equine friends. To symbolise the purpose of this altar, add a figure, picture or poster of a horse, preferably a white one, or perhaps a lucky horseshoe. You can also use images of unicorns and winged horses. Other things you might like to include are any rosettes you may have won in local horse shows, a hoof pick, a well loved copy of *Black Beauty* or your favourite horse poem.

- Once your altar is set up, light the candles and speak the following charm three times:

Sweet Epona, hear my words,
Guardian goddess of the wild herds,
Creature of dreams, magnificent steed,
Of galloping hooves and equine speed.
Protect all horses, far and near;
Guard them from cruelty, pain and fear;
Give them instead lush grass to eat,
Sweet carrots to nibble, hay at their feet.
If they must be in service let their owner be true,
Bringing kind words, caresses and devotion too.
If sadly neglected let freedom be found;
Let them gallop away, on legs strong and sound.
To horses the world over, both captive and free,
I offer my love and my thanks to thee.
Goddess Epona, hear now my spell,
Let all horses be happy, healthy and well.

- Spend the rest of your day with horses, or reading about Epona or horses in general, or you could watch a film about horses, such as *Black Beauty, The Silver Brumbie* or *The Horse Whisperer.*
- Leave your altar set up for 24 hours, then give thanks to Epona and clear away your things.

Prosperity Chant

As the moon is waxing again, we can continue to work on our prosperity magic. This prosperity chant can be used any time you're working towards abundance, or as an affirmation if you find yourself worrying about money. Pine oil is great for its money-drawing properties, so you might like to have some in an oil burner or burn some pine incense sticks. As you chant this spell, you can also light and focus on a green candle if you wish.

Money come to me, come to me, come to me.
Abundance set me free, set me free, set me free.
Poverty and debt, leave me be, leave me be.
Prosperity for all, let it be, let it be.

Repeat this chant as often as you like.

January

Dawn 07.59
Dusk 16.10

Monday 2nd

Moon quarter	1st (waxing)	Herb or incense	Fennel
Moon sign	♒	Crystal	Kunzite
Colour	Blue	Sun sign	♑

Tuesday 3rd

Moon quarter	1st (waxing)	Crystal	Amethyst
Moon sign	♒ 12.43 ♓	Sun sign	♑
Colour	Pink	Special	21.26 Mercury ☿ enters Capricorn ♑
Herb or incense	Thyme		

Wednesday 4th

Moon quarter	1st (waxing)	Herb or incense	Borage
Moon sign	♓	Crystal	Sodalite
Colour	Orange	Sun sign	♑

Thursday 5th

Moon quarter	1st (waxing)	Herb or incense	Valerian
Moon sign	♓ 14.44 ♈	Crystal	Aventurine
Colour	Jade	Sun sign	♑

Friday 6th

Moon phase	◐	Herb or incense	Rosemary
Time	18.56	Crystal	Topaz
Moon quarter	2nd (waxing)	Sun sign	♑
Moon sign	♈	Special	Twelfth Night Wassail Eve
Colour	Peach		

Saturday 7th

Moon quarter	2nd (waxing)	Herb or incense	Bayberry
Moon sign	♈ 09.09 ♉	Crystal	Amber
Colour	Indigo	Sun sign	♑

Sunday 8th

Moon quarter	2nd (waxing)	Herb or incense	Catnip
Moon sign	♉	Crystal	Jasper
Colour	Black	Sun sign	♑

January

Dawn 07.57
Dusk 16.16

Monday 9th			
Moon quarter	2nd (waxing)	Herb or incense	Mugwort
Moon sign	♉	Crystal	Tiger's Eye
Colour	Green	Sun sign	♑

Tuesday 10th			
Moon quarter	2nd (waxing)	Herb or incense	Mint
Moon sign	♉ 01.58 ♊	Crystal	Carnelian
Colour	Brown	Sun sign	♑

Wednesday 11th			
Moon quarter	2nd (waxing)	Herb or incense	Jasmine
Moon sign	♊	Crystal	Rose Quartz
Colour	Red	Sun sign	♑

Thursday 12th			
Moon quarter	2nd (waxing)	Herb or incense	Ginger
Moon sign	♊ 10.50 ♋	Crystal	Hematite
Colour	Yellow	Sun sign	♑

Friday 13th			
Moon quarter	2nd (waxing)	Herb or incense	Mace
Moon sign	♋	Crystal	Smoky Quartz
Colour	Grey	Sun sign	♑

Saturday 14th			
Moon phase	○	Herb or incense	Dill
Time	09.48	Crystal	Moonstone
Moon quarter	3rd (waning)	Sun sign	♑
Moon sign	♋ 21.31 ♌	Special	Wolf Moon
Colour	Purple		

Sunday 15th			
Moon quarter	3rd (waning)	Herb or incense	Cinnamon
Moon sign	♌	Crystal	Snowy Quartz
Colour	Green	Sun sign	♑

WOLF MOON

The full moon falls on January 14th. In addition to working a full moon ritual, many witches use this time to attune with power animals. A power animal is the astral essence of a particular animal with which you feel an affinity, and there is no limit to the number of power animals you can work with.

The full moon of January is traditionally known as the wolf moon. In days gone by, when wolves roamed freely, they would come in from the wilderness at this time in search of food. As a result the wolf came to be seen as an indiscriminate killer. Thankfully we have now progressed beyond such superstition and can see the wolf for what it is – a beautiful, magnificent and highly intelligent animal.

Witches have long used the energies of wolves during ritual. They can be called upon for strength, integrity, nurturing, loyalty or, as in the case of the spell below, for protection.

Wolf Moon Spell

You can use this spell to protect you at any time, although the third quarter is a good time, or you can adapt it to have the wolf patrol your property, guarding it like a magical night watch dog!

Purpose of ritual: to seek protection through the energies of the wolf

- Cast the Circle in the usual way and perform any full moon magic.
- When you have finished your other work, close your eyes and visualise a wolf before you. He can be any colour you like, but personally I visualise my wolf as the darkest midnight black, with glowing amber eyes. If you find it difficult to hold the visualisation then use a picture of a wolf that appeals to you and focus on that. Pictures from old calendars, cut out and mounted in clip frames, make fabulous and inexpensive power animal pictures.
- Once you can see the wolf clearly in your mind's eye, say:

Mighty wolf, I honour thee
And call you to this place.
I ask that you protect me,
Within this time and space.

Guard me close with tooth and claw,
Shield me from all harm.
Fear and fright I know no more,
Your wolf strength keeps me calm.
Snap and snarl at those who seem
Intent on being my foe.
Creature of my witchcraft dream,
Protect me with your wolf patrol.

- Imagine that the wolf patrols your Circle three times and then dissolves from view. Know that your power animal will protect you from any who wish you harm.

SUN MOVES INTO AQUARIUS

January 20th is the first day of the sign Aquarius, the water bearer. Aquarius is ruled by Uranus and the birthstone for this month is the garnet, while the ruling stone is the kunzite – a purple stone that can be used to aid relaxation and diffuse frustration.

People born under the sign of Aquarius are very single-minded, occasionally to the point of being stubborn! However, their ability to see things through to the very end is flawless. They also have a thirst for knowledge and give all of themselves to their career and to their loved ones.

On the less positive side, Aquarians can sometimes be irresponsible and attract chaos and anarchy into their lives without even being aware of it. This can lead to feelings of aloneness and, in extreme cases, a victim mentality.

Characteristically, Aquarians are innovative individuals who strive for enlightenment.

January

Dawn 07.53
Dusk 16.25

Monday 16th			
Moon quarter	3rd (waning)	Herb or incense	Parsley
Moon sign	♌	Crystal	Citrine
Colour	White	Sun sign	♑

Tuesday 17th			
Moon quarter	3rd (waning)	Herb or incense	Valerian
Moon sign	♌ 09.49 ♍	Crystal	Snowflake-Obsidian
Colour	Gold	Sun sign	♑

Wednesday 18th			
Moon quarter	3rd (waning)	Herb or incense	Mint
Moon sign	♍	Crystal	Bloodstone
Colour	Blue	Sun sign	♑

Thursday 19th			
Moon quarter	3rd (waning)	Herb or incense	Sage
Moon sign	♍ 22.49 ♎	Crystal	Snowy Quartz
Colour	Red	Sun sign	♑

Friday 20th			
Moon quarter	3rd (waning)	Herb or incense	Angelica
Moon sign	♎	Crystal	Kunzite
Colour	Jade	Sun sign	♑ 05.15 ♒

Saturday 21st			
Moon quarter	3rd (waning)	Herb or incense	Nutmeg
Moon sign	♎	Crystal	Topaz
Colour	Yellow	Sun sign	♒

Sunday 22nd			
Moon phase	◑	Herb or incense	Fennel
Time	15.14	Crystal	Amber
Moon quarter	4th (waning)	Sun sign	♒
Moon sign	♎ 10.28 ♏	Special	20.41 Mercury ☿ enters Aquarius ♒
Colour	Indigo		

January

Dawn 07.46
Dusk 16.37

Monday 23rd			
Moon quarter	4th (waning)	Herb or incense	Jasmine
Moon sign	♏	Crystal	Hematite
Colour	Silver	Sun sign	♒

Tuesday 24th			
Moon quarter	4th (waning)	Herb or incense	Catnip
Moon sign	♏ 18.38 ♐	Crystal	Moonstone
Colour	White	Sun sign	♒

Wednesday 25th			
Moon quarter	4th (waning)	Herb or incense	Mint
Moon sign	♐	Crystal	Sodalite
Colour	Peach	Sun sign	♒

Thursday 26th			
Moon quarter	4th (waning)	Herb or incense	Sage
Moon sign	♐ 22.31 ♑	Crystal	Amethyst
Colour	Black	Sun sign	♒

Friday 27th			
Moon quarter	4th (waning)	Herb or incense	Ginger
Moon sign	♑	Crystal	Aventurine
Colour	Pink	Sun sign	♒

Saturday 28th			
Moon quarter	4th (waning)	Herb or incense	Bayberry
Moon sign	♑ 23.09 ♒	Crystal	Citrine
Colour	Brown	Sun sign	♒

Sunday 29th			
Moon phase	●	Herb or incense	Fennel
Time	14.15	Crystal	Tiger's Eye
Moon quarter	1st (waxing)	Sun sign	♒
Moon sign	♒	Special	Chinese New Year (year of the fire dog)
Colour	Gold		

Goal Visualisation

For this visualisation you will need the list of goals you wrote in your diary as part of the new year ritual. This is a mental exercise, so make sure you are sitting comfortably. You do not need to cast a Circle, but you might like to light candles and your favourite incense to create a meditative atmosphere.

Now look at your list of goals and pick out one in particular. Focus completely on the manifestation of that goal. Think positive. Don't think of anything that might be standing in your way; simply imagine yourself enjoying the goal as if it has already happened. How do you feel? How do you behave? How has your life changed now that this goal has been achieved? Spend as much time as you can just sitting and imagining that this goal is a reality and making a mental note of how that makes you feel.

Hold on to this feeling after you have finished the visualisation, and practise it again as often as you can. Magical visualisation is a vital tool in helping your goals to manifest and you should indulge in it whenever and wherever you can.

January

Dawn 07.38
Dusk 16.48

Monday 30th			
Moon quarter	1st (waxing)	Herb or incense	Dill
Moon sign	♒ 22.32 ♓	Crystal	Carnelian
Colour	Yellow	Sun sign	♒

Tuesday 31st			
Moon quarter	1st (waxing)	Herb or incense	Mace
Moon sign	♓	Crystal	Amber
Colour	Red	Sun sign	♒

Dream Lover

Can you see me now, my love,
Dancing through your dreams?
Do you feel me now, my love,
For nothing is what it seems?
A dream is a dream is a dream
Unless by magic guided;
A dream is a dream is a dream
Unless by witchcraft blinded.
See only me, my love,
Feel me in your arms.
Love only me, my love,
And taste of witch's charms.
My face swims in your dreams
As you close your tired eyes;
In sleep I make you mine,
My touch invokes your sighs.
Drink a sleeping draught, my love,
And stay a while longer;
The more you dream me real, my love,
The more my power grows stronger.
Bring me forth from sleep, my love,
And look for me in life.
Your heart I vow to keep,
My love cuts deeper than a knife.
Only you can pull me forth
And bring me into being.
In life, I'm right before you, love,
Open your eyes – start seeing.

February

During the month of February the days begin to lengthen and we see the light gradually growing stronger as we move into the year. Spring is approaching, though at the moment the days are still cold and may even bring flurries of snow. Deep in the womb of the earth, new life begins to stir and the sap of trees slowly starts to rise. All of this is hidden from our view of course, but a bunch of snowdrops pushing through the soil tells us that winter is almost over and the lighter half of the year is ahead.

The Celts associated this month with the willow tree, or saille, as they would call it. This tree was seen as feminine in terms of energy and was linked to the moon and the lunar cycle. In Celtic tradition women were held in high esteem and often took on powerful roles such as priestess, prophet or warrior. Symbolically, the willow tree denotes spiritual balance, fertility and the general flow of all life. Its wood is often used to make magical tools such as wands, staffs and sets of runes.

In the language of flowers, the plant associated with February is the iris, symbolic of hope. At this time of year we feel hope that the winter is finished and the warmer days of spring and summer are fast approaching. A vase of irises looks lovely on a springtime altar. The herbs linked with this time are sage and ylang-ylang, so burning these will help you to attune with the season. February is also a time of cleansing, so sage smudge sticks are in keeping with this month.

February is probably best known for being the lover's month, as St Valentine's day is celebrated on the 14th. This is the perfect time of year to cast spells for love, make divinations concerning a future spouse, or set up a love altar. February is also the month of the witches' sabbat Imbolc.

IMBOLC

Traditionally, all witches' sabbats are celebrated from sunset to sunset, as the ancients believed that the setting sun signified the start of a day rather than the end, as the modern world views it. This is why most sabbats effectively span two days. This often works out well for modern witches, as it means that you can pick the day for your ritual that best fits into your life, taking all your other commitments into account.

Imbolc, also known as the festival of lights, is sacred to the goddess Brede. Also known as Bride, Brigid, Brigit and Brigantia, she is a goddess of many names. It is at this time that we welcome the growing light and lengthening days. The word Imbolc refers to the ewe's milk that once (before intensive farming) fed the new lambs at this time of year. The Christian name for this festival is Candlemas, as the church would bless its candles at this time.

The colour of this sabbat is white, which symbolises the lambs and the ewe's milk, as well as the forthcoming light. A nice tradition on this day is to turn on all the lights in the house in reflection of the strengthening sun. For the ritual itself, though, the magical area should be lit by candlelight alone, preferably lots of it, making the ritual night as bright as the day – it is a festival of light, after all!

The Imbolc altar should be draped with a white cloth, and white pillar candles should be placed on it. In addition, a vase of lilies, snowdrops or other white flowers should be used as decoration, and you might like to add white ribbons and bows. As the flower of February and symbol of hope, irises would also look lovely.

Another traditional sabbat decoration is Brede's bed. This is a small box or basket with pretty fabric laid within to form a bed. This should be placed on the hearth with a corn dolly, to represent Brede, inside it. Brede's bed is left in place throughout the festival, as this is said to invite all the blessings of the goddess into your home. The bed should be used for no other purpose but this rite and is brought out every Imbolc.

If you would like to add a little colour to this traditionally all-white sabbat, then use the Triple Goddess colours of red, white and black. Alternatively, you might like to add a lunar aspect to your ritual by including a dash of silver. Remember, though, that this is the feast of Brede, so keep your colours predominantly white in honour of this goddess and her time.

Sabbats always end with a feast, and Imbolc is no exception. Customary foods include rice pudding, sago, rice, milk, cornbreads and cakes, white meat and fish, eggs, yoghurt and cheeses.

Imbolc is also a time of cleansing, so a spring clean and clear out is appropriate, followed by a ritual smudging of your entire home with an incense made up of this month's herbs, sage and ylang-ylang. Alternatively, smudge with a sage stick and burn ylang-ylang oil in an oil burner. Imbolc is the traditional time to cleanse and reconsecrate your ritual tools. The ritual on page 69 describes how to do this.

February

Dawn 07.38
Dusk 16.48

Wednesday 1st			
Moon quarter	1st (waxing)	Herb or incense	Mint
Moon sign	♓ 22.46 ♈	Crystal	Clear Quartz
Colour	Yellow	Sun sign	♒

Thursday 2nd			
Moon quarter	1st (waxing)	Crystal	Sodalite
Moon sign	♈	Sun sign	♒
Colour	Silver	Special	Imbolc
Herb or incense	Sage		

Friday 3rd			
Moon quarter	1st (waxing)	Herb or incense	Dill
Moon sign	♈	Crystal	Kunzite
Colour	Orange	Sun sign	♒

Saturday 4th			
Moon quarter	1st (waxing)	Herb or incense	Borage
Moon sign	♈ 01.31 ♉	Crystal	Carnelian
Colour	Jade	Sun sign	♒

Sunday 5th			
Moon phase	◐	Colour	Pink
Time	06.29	Herb or incense	Mugwort
Moon quarter	2nd (waxing)	Crystal	Citrine
Moon sign	♉	Sun sign	♒

Imbolc Ritual

Purpose of ritual: to honour the goddess Brede and cleanse your tools
What you need: all your ritual tools, candles, incense, salt, a bowl of water

- After dressing the altar, putting Brede's bed in place and preparing the sabbat feast, cast the Circle, calling on Brede and giving her honour and thanks. If you want to invoke guardians, perform a quarter call after casting the Circle.
- Light the candles and incense and perform the following invocation:

Here is Imbolc, feast of flames;
Winter ends as sunlight gains.
Goddess Brede, I call you here;
Bring the Sun God, strong and clear.
Goddess of so many names,
We welcome you as winter wanes.
Lay your blessings beside Brede's bed;
It is the Old Ways we now tred.
Power now to us reveal,
With the turning of the wheel.

- Now take out all your ritual tools and magically cleanse and consecrate them by passing each one through the four elements. Sprinkle each tool first with salt to represent Earth and then with water. Now carefully pass it over a candle flame and through the smoke of burning incense. As you do this, say:

I cleanse and consecrate this ----- and dedicate it to the Goddess and the God. Blessed Be!

- Finally, perform any magical spells or divinations you have planned and then enjoy the sabbat feast! Don't forget to release any quarters and take down the Circle afterwards.

To Strengthen Love

Purpose of ritual: to strengthen the bond between lovers
What you need: jewellery belonging to you and to your partner (wedding rings are ideal), your pentacle

- Place both pieces of jewellery on the pentacle. Hold your hands over the pentacle and visualise a stream of warm pink light coming from your palms and being absorbed by the jewellery.
- Now say:

With this spell our love will be
A bond so strong for all to see.

- Continue this chant for as long as your visualisation remains clear.
- When you have finished the ritual, you and your partner should both wear the jewellery to connect you with the magic.

Self-nurturing Ritual

This ritual is for all you single people out there who could do with a little indulgence and self-love around Valentine's day or at any time.

Purpose of ritual: to foster self-love
What you need: a large bottle of pure spring water, your cauldron, rock and sea salts, three pink roses, your favourite essential oil, your wand

- Pour the bottle of pure spring water into your cauldron. Add a teaspoon of rock salt, a teaspoon of sea salt and the petals of three pink roses. Finally, add five drops of the essential oil.
- Stir the mixture with your wand, envisaging the soft pink light of self-love being absorbed by the potion.
- Run a hot bath and pour the potion into the bath water just before getting in. Lie back and relax, allowing the essential oils to soothe you. (If you don't have a bath, you can spritz yourself with the potion in a nice warm shower.)
- Finish your ritual with a night of indulgence – watch your favourite movie while eating a takeaway, sipping champagne and dipping into a box of luxury chocolates! Who says being single means being miserable on Valentine's day?

February

Dawn 07.28
Dusk 17.00

Monday 6th			
Moon quarter	2nd (waxing)	Herb or incense	Catnip
Moon sign	♉ 07.13 ♊	Crystal	Topaz
Colour	Purple	Sun sign	♒

Tuesday 7th			
Moon quarter	2nd (waxing)	Herb or incense	Dill
Moon sign	♊	Crystal	Hematite
Colour	Green	Sun sign	♒

Wednesday 8th			
Moon quarter	2nd (waxing)	Herb or incense	Sage
Moon sign	♊ 16.33 ♋	Crystal	Obsidian
Colour	White	Sun sign	♒

Thursday 9th			
Moon quarter	2nd (waxing)	Crystal	Amber
Moon sign	♋	Sun sign	♒
Colour	Brown	Special	01.22 Mercury ☿ enters Pisces ♓
Herb or incense	Parsley		

Friday 10th			
Moon quarter	2nd (waxing)	Herb or incense	Thyme
Moon sign	♋	Crystal	Rose Quartz
Colour	Black	Sun sign	♒

Saturday 11th			
Moon quarter	2nd (waxing)	Herb or incense	Pine
Moon sign	♋ 03.44 ♌	Crystal	Aventurine
Colour	Gold	Sun sign	♒

Sunday 12th			
Moon quarter	2nd (waxing)	Herb or incense	Lavender
Moon sign	♌	Crystal	Carnelian
Colour	Grey	Sun sign	♒

STORM MOON

The full moon of February falls on Monday 13th and is known as the storm moon, so this is a great time to work protection spells to guard your home against bad weather. A good way to protect against storm damage and lightning strikes is to call on the aid of the salamanders. Do this by lighting a bright red or orange candle. Sit before it for a few minutes, concentrating on the flame, and then say these words or ones of your own devising:

I call the salamanders, spirits of fire. I ask that you protect this home and all within from lightning strikes and all forms of destructive fire. May we continue to enjoy the warmth and comfort of your flames, without the danger. I close this spell in thanks. Blessed be!

Allow the candle to burn down in honour of the salamanders and place a figure of a dragon or lizard on your hearth.

VALENTINE'S DAY

The world is filled with romance and every high street store sells hearts and flowers, cards and cakes. But is there more to Valentine's day than a commercialised attempt at cashing in on our emotions? Absolutely! Like many commercialised festivals, Valentine's day actually has echoes of old Pagan traditions. If we want to revive these traditions, we simply have to realise that February 14th is a festival of love – all love, not just the romantic variety! So use this day to tell those close to you just what they really mean to you.

The Pagan roots of Valentine's day lie within a festival originally called Lupercalia, which was celebrated on February 15th and was sacred to the god Lupercus. Like Valentine's day, it was a festival of love and also of fertility.

Many traditional Valentine's symbols are actually Pagan in origin. Take the cute little cherubs that adorn modern Valentine's day cards. These represent the Greek Cupid (Roman Eros), god of love and son of the goddess of love and beauty, Aphrodite (Venus). And even the depiction of love hearts has its foundation in an ancient Norse rune dedicated to and symbolising sex!

Dawn 07.16 Dusk 17.15

Monday 13th

Moon phase	○	Herb or incense	Mace
Time	04.44	Crystal	Snowflake-Obsidian
Moon quarter	3rd (waning)	Sun sign	♒
Moon sign	♌ 16.13 ♍	Special	Storm Moon
Colour	White		Witchcraft Act repealed 1951

Tuesday 14th

Moon quarter	3rd (waning)	Crystal	Carnelian
Moon sign	♍	Sun sign	♒
Colour	Red	Special	Valentine's Day
Herb or incense	Rosemary		

Wednesday 15th

Moon quarter	3rd (waning)	Crystal	Jasper
Moon sign	♍ 05.09 ♎	Sun sign	♒
Colour	Green	Special	Lupercalia
Herb or incense	Cinnamon		

Thursday 16th

Moon quarter	3rd (waning)	Herb or incense	Parsley
Moon sign	♎	Crystal	Amber
Colour	Blue	Sun sign	♒

Friday 17th

Moon quarter	3rd (waning)	Crystal	Topaz
Moon sign	♎	Sun sign	♒
Colour	Indigo	Special	22.44 Mars ♂
Herb or incense	Valerian		enters Gemini ♊

Saturday 18th

Moon quarter	3rd (waning)	Herb or incense	Angelica
Moon sign	♎ 17.11 ♏	Crystal	Sodalite
Colour	Peach	Sun sign	♒ 19.26 ♓

Sunday 19th

Moon quarter	3rd (waning)	Herb or incense	Nutmeg
Moon sign	♏	Crystal	Bloodstone
Colour	Brown	Sun sign	♓

SUN MOVES INTO PISCES

The Sun moves into Pisces on February 18th. If you were born under the sign of Pisces, your ruling planet is Neptune, giving you an affinity with water – after all, this is the sign of the fish. Your ruling stone is the opal and your birthstone is the amethyst. Both of these could be used in your magic or worn as talismans. Pisceans are known for their deep understanding and can turn their minds to most things with success. They have a deep empathy with people and so do well in careers that make the most of this quality, such as care work and holistic medicine.

On the negative side, Pisceans often live life on an emotional rollercoaster, constantly switching between euphoria and deep despair. This can lead to feelings of confusion, and may make them difficult to understand and hard to live with. However, at their best Pisceans are sympathetic to others, caring, considerate, artistic and creative, with a strong intuitive sense of other people's feelings.

Valentine's Day Ritual

Your Lupercalian/Valentine's altar should be decorated with the seasonal colours of red, pink and the deep lilac of Lupercalia. Add sweet-smelling flowers, particularly roses, the flower of love. For a ritual carried out at this time, you might like to burn floral oil or incense and play soft music – harp music, the music of the cherubs, is particularly appropriate. Champagne, white and red wine, strawberries, grapes and, of course, special chocolates should form your ritual feast.

Cauldron of Transformation

In Celtic mythology the cauldron is a tool of transformation, healing the sick, bestowing eternal youth and beauty, and even bringing dead warriors back to life. While your own cauldron won't be quite as powerful, you can still use its symbolism in your spells. This time, just before the new moon, is great for working magic to help you overcome bad habits and banish things from your life. This spell is best performed outdoors.

Purpose of ritual: to remove a negative habit
What you need: a cauldron, dried sage and basil, sand, a charcoal block, matches, a pen, a piece of paper

- Place your cauldron before you and pour a little sand into the bottom of it to absorb the heat.
- Write your negative habit, or whatever it is you would like to change about your life, on the paper.
- Light a charcoal block and place this in the cauldron on the bed of sand. Then light the spell paper and add that too.
- Once the paper has burned away, sprinkle in a small amount of dried sage and the power herb basil. Say these words:

Sage to cleanse and basil to send,
This negative pattern is now at an end.

- Watch as the cauldron transforms your bad habit into dust and ashes.
- Leave the cauldron outdoors to cool and go about your normal day.

Spell to Find Love

Purpose of spell: to bring a lover into your life
What you need: a red candle, your favourite essential oil, a pen, a piece of paper

- Take a red candle and anoint it with the essential oil.
- Write a list of all that you want in a lover and companion. Fold the list carefully.
- Light the candle and speak this charm three times:

With these words this spell I sow.
Bring the love I've yet to know.
Fill my heart and set it a-glow,
Secrets only witches know.
I take the power and let it go.
As I will, it shall be so!

- Burn the spell paper and wait for your love to come to you.

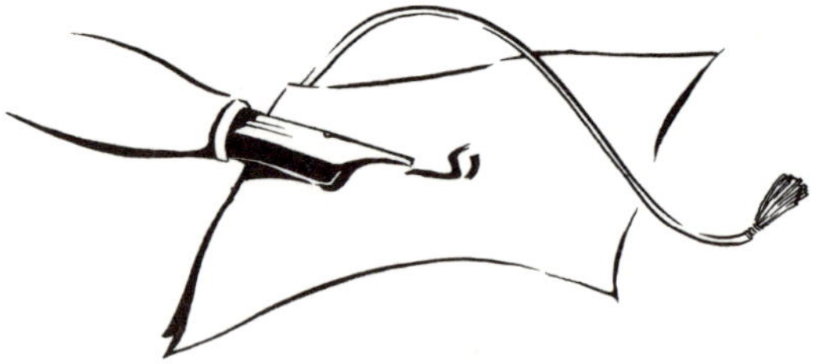

February

Dawn 07.04
Dusk 17.21

Monday 20th			
Moon quarter	3rd (waning)	Herb or incense	Rosemary
Moon sign	♏	Crystal	Citrine
Colour	Red	Sun sign	♓

Tuesday 21st			
Moon phase	◑	Colour	Pink
Time	07.17	Herb or incense	Valerian
Moon quarter	4th (waning)	Crystal	Rose Quartz
Moon sign	♏ 02.38 ♐	Sun sign	♓

Wednesday 22nd			
Moon quarter	4th (waning)	Herb or incense	Dill
Moon sign	♐	Crystal	Kunzite
Colour	Indigo	Sun sign	♓

Thursday 23rd			
Moon quarter	4th (waning)	Herb or incense	Mace
Moon sign	♐ 08.16 ♑	Crystal	Hematite
Colour	Purple	Sun sign	♓

Friday 24th			
Moon quarter	4th (waning)	Herb or incense	Borage
Moon sign	♑	Crystal	Obsidian
Colour	Jade	Sun sign	♓

Saturday 25th			
Moon quarter	4th (waning)	Herb or incense	Angelica
Moon sign	♑ 10.14 ♒	Crystal	Jasper
Colour	Gold	Sun sign	♓

Sunday 26th			
Moon quarter	4th (waning)	Herb or incense	Fennel
Moon sign	♒	Crystal	Bloodstone
Colour	Brown	Sun sign	♓

Household Cleansing Ritual

If you didn't perform a cleansing as part of your Imbolc celebrations, then you should do one now. The best way to attract wonderful new things into your life is to do away with all the old junk you don't need! This creates space for all your material goals to manifest. So begin by having a huge clear-out, throwing away anything that is broken or useless, and giving anything in good condition that you no longer want to a charity shop. Once all the clutter is cleared, go around your home and clean it thoroughly with a duster and hoover. If you like, add a few drops of lemon juice and grapefruit essential oil to your cleaning water, as these will give off an uplifting fragrance which is good for both yourself and your home! Next, open all the windows, put on some soothing music and begin the ritual cleansing.

Purpose of ritual: to clear your home of negative energy
What you need: some pure spring water, a small bowl, lavender essential oil, rock and sea salts, your wand or athame, a bell or windchimes, a scented candle

- Pour a little of the spring water into a small bowl. Add two drops of lavender essential oil, one pinch of rock salt and one pinch of sea salt. Stir the mixture with your wand or athame in a deosil (clockwise) direction.
- Go around your home, again in a deosil direction, and sprinkle the cleansing mixture around each room. As you go repeat this sentence:

I cleanse this space.

- Take a stick of your favourite incense, light it and move it around the perimeter of all doorways and windows, cleansing and sealing them with the fragrant smoke.
- Make a third trip all around the house, this time with either a bell or windchimes, cleansing each room with the power of sound.
- Your space is now clean, clear of clutter and magically cleansed. Finish off by lighting a scented candle and relaxing quietly.

Monday 27th			
Moon quarter	4th (waning)	Herb or incense	Pine
Moon sign	♒ 09.56 ♓	Crystal	Carnelian
Colour	Silver	Sun sign	♓

Dawn 06.50
Dusk 17.36

Tuesday 28th			
Moon phase	●	Colour	Silver
Time	00.31	Herb or incense	Mint
Moon quarter	1st (waxing)	Crystal	Amber
Moon sign	♓	Sun sign	♓

Sowing the Seeds of Dreams

It is the time of year for seeds to be sown, so that we can enjoy the bounty of the harvest later on. In this little ritual, we sow the seeds of dreams, so choose seeds of flowers that really speak to you – perhaps the flower associated with your month of birth.

Purpose of ritual: to magically sow your dreams
What you need: flower seeds, your pentacle, a bedding tray, soil, your athame, water, plant food

- Put the seeds to charge on your pentacle.
- Fill the bedding tray with soil.
- Think of one of your goals – something you would really like to achieve – and, using your athame, write a single word in the soil that totally sums up your dream.
- Carefully plant the flower seeds into the soil word, so that as they grow they spell out your dream, and your dream will grow with them.
- Hold your hands over the tray, sending your love and energy into the seeds and willing them to grow strong and true.
- Cover the seeds with soil, being careful not to destroy the word you have made and then add a little water and plant food to give the them a good start.
- Tend the seeds carefully to ensure the flowering of your goal.

The Maiden

I am the Maiden;
I am the spring;
I am the laughter that awakens all things.
I am the crocus,
The daffodils in bloom,
Weaving sunlight and rainbows at the magical loom.
Mine is the step,
That awakens the Earth;
I am the Goddess of joy and rebirth.
Mine is the song
Of the butterfly wings;
I am the voice as creation sings.
I am seduction,
Love and romance,
The Goddess who mates with the Lord of the Dance.
I am a vision,
Of wonder, delight.
Step into my world and embrace the new light.

March

As the world begins to warm up, there is a definite feeling of spring in the air. The trees bear branches full of buds, waiting to burst into leaf and blossom. Crocus flowers peek out from their sheltered banks, and a pale sun climbs the sky, growing stronger day by day. The temperature is still low and the rain showers us every now and then.

There is a quickening in the earth as life renews itself for another cycle. This is the time of rebirth, the month of the spring equinox, the sabbat of Ostara. It is also the season of Robin Hood and his bride, Maid Marian. During this season we call upon this aspect of the God and Goddess and attune with the essence of their myth, reliving the old tales to find the truth behind them and strengthen our own courage.

To the Celts, the tree that symbolised this month was the ash tree, or nuin. The ash represented the cosmic world tree, connecting all things and all aspects of life. It linked the Underworld, the Otherworld and our own world, represented the three realms of Past, Present and Future, and linked the microcosm and macrocosm. The wisdom of the ash tree teaches us that we are all linked in the circle of life and represents the Pagan belief 'as above, so below'.

The wood of the ash was used extensively by the Druids, and with the oak and hawthorn it makes up the faery triad of oak, ash and thorn. It is said that where these three trees grow together, the land is filled with magic and power, and a gateway to the faery realms is nearby.

The flower of March is, of course, the daffodil. A flurry of saffron and gold is scattered over the earth as these beautiful flowers come into bloom. Their fragrance is warm and strong, and they are a true sign of spring. In the language of flowers the daffodil stands for chivalry, which links it to this season of Robin Hood.

The herbs associated with March are cinnamon and – the most powerful herb of all – dragon's blood. These dried herbs can be mixed and burnt as an incense, or scattered around the garden in a rite of protection. You could write your Book of Shadows with dragon's blood ink, burn dragon's blood oil or add cinnamon to your cooking.

March

Dawn 06.50 Dusk 17.36

Wednesday 1st			
Moon quarter	1st (waxing)	Herb or incense	Borage
Moon sign	♓ 09.19 ♈	Crystal	Amethyst
Colour	Jade	Sun sign	♓

Thursday 2nd			
Moon quarter	1st (waxing)	Herb or incense	Mace
Moon sign	♈	Crystal	Sodalite
Colour	Orange	Sun sign	♓

Friday 3rd			
Moon quarter	1st (waxing)	Herb or incense	Angelica
Moon sign	♈ 10.22 ♉	Crystal	Smokey Quartz
Colour	Brown	Sun sign	♓

Saturday 4th			
Moon quarter	1st (waxing)	Herb or incense	Dill
Moon sign	♉	Crystal	Jasper
Colour	Black	Sun sign	♓

Sunday 5th			
Moon quarter	1st (waxing)	Crystal	Carnelian
Moon sign	♉ 14.38 ♊	Sun sign	♓
Colour	Grey	Special	08.39 Venus ♀ enters Aquarius ♒
Herb or incense	Thyme		

To Decorate a Broom

Purpose of ritual: to decorate a broom
What you need: a broom; things to decorate it with such as ribbons, beads, feathers, bells, pine cones, decorative glass berries and leaves, crystals, sea shells, etc.

- Decorating a broom, or besom as it is also called, is a traditional pastime for a witch. This creative activity links our personal energies with the broom as a magical tool. It also ensures our magic remains individual to us as we spend time personalising our tools.
- A traditional witch's broom should be made from heather and, although these can be quite expensive, they are well worth the expense as they don't shed their twigs all over the place!
- You can use a variety of things to decorate your broom, including ribbons, beads, feathers, bells, pine cones, decorative glass berries and leaves, crystals, sea shells and so on. This is a great time to let your imagination run wild, so visit any craft shop and pick up whatever takes your fancy.
- Traditionally, each of the four elements should be represented on the broom and the easiest way to do this is to use coloured ribbons: green for Earth, yellow for Air, red for Fire and blue for Water. It is also usual to write your magical name on the stave of the broom – though you could disguise this by writing the name in Norse runes or even Elven runes if you prefer. Use paints, pens or stickers to do this, or for a more permanent and professional finish, use a wood burning tool.
- Finally, bless the newly-decorated broom by sprinkling it with rose water and saying:

  'I bless this besom as a tool of my magic. So mote it be.'
- Your magical broom is now ready to use in your rituals.

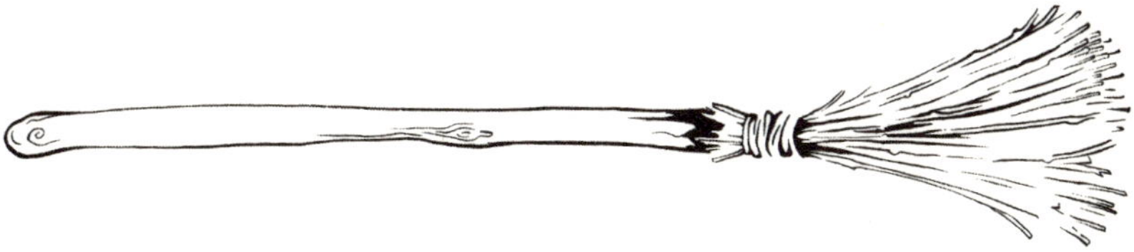

Marian's Love Spell

Purpose of ritual: to attune with Maid Marian and find love

What you need: an item of nature to represent each element (for example, a feather for Air, a shell for Water, a bright red or yellow flower for Fire, a twig for Earth), a representation of Maid Marian, a small plate or trinket box, a sprinkling of confetti, a red envelope

- Place all your natural objects neatly on the plate or in the trinket box.
- Concentrating on the image of Maid Marian, invoke her help by saying the following charm:

I call on Marian, Queen of the wood,
Companion and wife of Robin Hood,
Known among witches as Queen of the May.
I invoke your assistance here this day.
Take these gifts of forest floor;
Bring true love to my door.
Lady of leaf, bud and flower,
Send me a lover, heed my power.

- Sprinkle the confetti over the natural objects and leave them on your altar for three days.
- When three days have passed, seal the natural objects in the red envelope and wait for love to come to you.

March

Dawn 06.36
Dusk 17.48

Monday 6th

Moon phase	◐	Colour	Yellow
Time	20.16	Herb or incense	Bayberry
Moon quarter	2nd (waxing)	Crystal	Clear Quartz
Moon sign	♊	Sun sign	♓

Tuesday 7th

Moon quarter	2nd (waxing)	Herb or incense	Bay
Moon sign	♊ 22.38 ♋	Crystal	Topaz
Colour	Indigo	Sun sign	♓

Wednesday 8th

Moon quarter	2nd (waxing)	Crystal	Sodalite
Moon sign	♋	Sun sign	♓
Colour	Purple	Special	International
Herb or incense	Mugwort		Women's Day

Thursday 9th

Moon quarter	2nd (waxing)	Herb or incense	Sage
Moon sign	♋	Crystal	Carnelian
Colour	Silver	Sun sign	♓

Friday 10th

Moon quarter	2nd (waxing)	Herb or incense	Fennel
Moon sign	♋ 09.42 ♌	Crystal	Topaz
Colour	Green	Sun sign	♓

Saturday 11th

Moon quarter	2nd (waxing)	Herb or incense	Valerian
Moon sign	♌	Crystal	Hematite
Colour	Blue	Sun sign	♓

Sunday 12th

Moon quarter	2nd (waxing)	Herb or incense	Cinnamon
Moon sign	♌ 22.24 ♍	Crystal	Topaz
Colour	Peach	Sun sign	♓

March

Dawn 06.21
Dusk 18.00

Monday 13th

Moon quarter	2nd (waxing)	Herb or incense	Parsley
Moon sign	♍	Crystal	Citrine
Colour	White	Sun sign	♓

Tuesday 14th

Moon phase	○	Herb or incense	Nutmeg
Time	23.35	Crystal	Moonstone
Moon quarter	3rd (waning)	Sun sign	♓
Moon sign	♍	Special	Chaste Moon
Colour	Pink		

Wednesday 15th

Moon quarter	3rd (waning)	Herb or incense	Ginger
Moon sign	♍ 11.12 ♎	Crystal	Citrine
Colour	Yellow	Sun sign	♓

Thursday 16th

Moon quarter	3rd (waning)	Herb or incense	Mugwort
Moon sign	♎	Crystal	Aventurine
Colour	Gold	Sun sign	♓

Friday 17th

Moon quarter	3rd (waning)	Herb or incense	Borage
Moon sign	♎ 22.59 ♏	Crystal	Bloodstone
Colour	Indigo	Sun sign	♓

Saturday 18th

Moon quarter	3rd (waning)	Herb or incense	Fennel
Moon sign	♏	Crystal	Topaz
Colour	Black	Sun sign	♓

Sunday 19th

Moon quarter	3rd (waning)	Crystal	Amber
Moon sign	♏	Sun sign	♓
Colour	Jade	Special	First recorded solar eclipse 721 BC
Herb or incense	Pine		

CHASTE MOON

The full moon of March is known as the chaste moon. This is an excellent time to work spells of self-acceptance if you are single, or to make a declaration to wait for true love if you have tumbled from one disastrous relationship to another. Either of these spells could be a part of your full moon esbat ritual.

SUN MOVES INTO ARIES

The sun now moves into the sign of Aries, which is ruled by Mars. This rulership gives those born under this sign quite a volatile edge, as Mars is the god of war. The power stone of Aries is the ruby, and the birth stone is the beautiful aquamarine. Both stones can be used in magical spells or worn as talismans. As a sign that represents new beginnings, Aries is deeply linked to the spring, and those born under this sign may find that this is their most productive time of the year.

At their worst, Aries people may be aggressive, with a slightly dismissive nature and a tendency to bully those weaker than themselves. At their best, though, they are courageous, show qualities of outstanding leadership and tend to have a very positive outlook on life.

OSTARA

Ostara is one of the sabbats and is the witches' name for the spring, or vernal, equinox. Although the date of the spring equinox varies from year to year, it always falls between March 21st and 23rd. At this time, night and day are of equal length, and from now on the hours of daylight will gradually increase.

Ostara was moved forwards in the Christian calendar and is celebrated as Easter, a spring festival that most people are familiar with. There are many similarities between these two celebrations, largely because the early Christians borrowed heavily from Pagan rites in order to convert the masses. For this reason, a Wiccan altar will probably look very similar to a church altar at this time.

For ostara, we decorate the altar with spring flowers and pretty candles, arranged over an altar cloth of a springtime colour such as lemon-yellow or mint-green. To this we add a profusion of highly decorated eggs, either the chocolate variety or hardboiled and hand-painted. Eggs symbolise the new life of spring. A decorative plate filled with different seeds can also be added to the altar – sunflower seeds, sesame seeds, flower seeds and so on – or seeds can simply be scattered over the altar cloth, like confetti. Images of chicks and lambs, creatures that sum up the spirit of the season and symbolise new life, are also appropriate decorations.

Some representation of a hare should always be placed on an ostara altar in order to invoke the blessings of fertility, growth and fruitfulness. Figures, paintings, postcards, wood carvings and magical moon hare statues (available from occult stores) all have a place on the ostara altar. The hare has long been associated with magic and witchcraft, and the easter bunny, loved by children everywhere, is its cousin, so add images of rabbits if you like.

Just why the hare and the rabbit are so closely linked with magic is unclear. It may be that their fertility cycle linked them with the moon and the seasons, and thus with magic. In medieval times, it was thought that a witch had the ability to shapeshift into a hare and so escape her accusers (at a time when witches were demonised and often killed). The Anglo-Saxon goddess Eostre, after whom the sabbat of ostara is named, was sometimes depicted with the head of a hare.

Your sabbat feast should include chocolate eggs, boiled eggs, milk puddings, egg custard, hot cross buns, seed breads, meringue nests and so on. Chicken, rabbit and lamb are also appropriate if your diet includes meat

A traditional activity for this sabbat is to paint eggs for your altar. These can be wooden eggs bought from a craft shop, or you can use hardboiled eggs and make new ones every year – this is especially useful if you have children to occupy! Use paints, glitter glue, nail polish, sequins, wood varnish and so on. Let the eggs dry overnight and then arrange them on your altar.

As this sabbat is about fertility and growth, any magic cast should be for the steady progression and fruitfulness of projects and ventures. Create your sabbat ritual to reflect your own life and your own goals, using the rituals in this book as a blueprint.

Shades of Sherwood

Purpose of ritual: a general fertility spell – yours to direct

What you need: five different leaves (these should be quite large, so oak, sycamore, holly, laurel and horse chestnut are all good); your pentacle; a black marker pen; an offering pouch of nuts, seeds and raisins, etc.

- Set the leaves to charge on your pentacle until you begin your magical work, at sunset.
- Write your goal on all five leaves with the black marker.
- Take the leaves back to the woods, or maybe to a magical place within your garden, and, kneeling down, silently ask Robin Hood and the Green Man to assist you in achieving this goal.
- Dig a small hole and lay your leaves carefully in it; add a couple of seeds to symbolise the fertility of your plans, and fill in the hole.
- Sit quietly for a few moments, giving thanks for all that you already have, then empty your offering pouch for the wildlife to enjoy. This is your gift to nature – to give is to receive, and this small, selfless act will complete the natural exchange of energy.
- Walk home, enjoying the evening and knowing that your magic is now in motion.

March

Dawn 06.05
Dusk 18.10

Monday 20th			
Moon quarter	3rd (waning)	Crystal	Jasper
Moon sign	♏ 08.43 ♐	Sun sign	♓ 18.26 ♈
Colour	Indigo	Special	Ostara (spring equinox 18.26)
Herb or incense	Jasmine		

Tuesday 21st			
Moon quarter	3rd (waning)	Herb or incense	Rosemary
Moon sign	♐	Crystal	Kunzite
Colour	Yellow	Sun sign	♈

Wednesday 22nd			
Moon phase	◑	Colour	Blue
Time	19.10	Herb or incense	Mint
Moon quarter	4th (waning)	Crystal	Aventurine
Moon sign	♐ 15.36 ♑	Sun sign	♈

Thursday 23rd			
Moon quarter	4th (waning)	Herb or incense	Thyme
Moon sign	♑	Crystal	Citrine
Colour	Silver	Sun sign	♈

Friday 24th			
Moon quarter	4th (waning)	Herb or incense	Valerian
Moon sign	♑ 19.21 ♒	Crystal	Tiger's Eye
Colour	Pink	Sun sign	♈

Saturday 25th			
Moon quarter	4th (waning)	Herb or incense	Lavender
Moon sign	♒	Crystal	Jasper
Colour	Peach	Sun sign	♈

Sunday 26th			
Moon quarter	4th (waning)	Crystal	Snowflake-Obsidian
Moon sign	♒ 20.23 ♓	Sun sign	♈
Colour	Indigo	Special	Mothering Sunday
Herb or incense	Mugwort		British Summer Time begins

Mother's Love Spell

Purpose of ritual: to give thanks for your mother's love
What you need: a photo of your mother, one red rose, one pink rose, two pink candles and holders, rosewood oil, a gift or flowers for your mother, a pink balloon, a pink ribbon, a pen, a small slip of paper

- Set up an altar dedicated to your mother and your love for one another. Place her photograph in the middle and surround it with a circle of red and pink rose petals. Place the gift or flowers nearby.
- Anoint the pink candles by rubbing the rosewood oil into the wax. Set them in holders on each side of the photo and light them.
- Sit for a while, thinking of your mother, of all that she's done for you and all that she means to you. Give thanks to the Goddess or your chosen divinity for the gift of your mother's love.
- Now think of a wish for your mum, a gift she'd like or something like improved health.
- Write the wish on a slip of paper, roll the paper into a scroll and pass it through the neck of the balloon. Add a couple of rose petals, blow up the balloon, tie a knot in the neck and attach the ribbon.
- Allow the candles to burn down, and complete the ritual by releasing the wish balloon into the air on the next windy day and presenting the gift to your mother.

Robin Hood's Spell for Courage

The trials of life can often leave us feeling weak and vulnerable to betrayal and abuse. Whenever you need to strengthen your defences and summon your courage, attune with Robin Hood by performing this spell.

Purpose of spell: to increase your courage
What you need: anything to do with Robin Hood: books, videos, statues and so on; a natural symbol of strength such as an oak leaf or acorn; pine incense (optional)

- Spend a little time getting reaquainted with the old myths of Robin Hood. As you read or watch, look beyond the stories to the magic and power of the God behind, remembering that Robin Hood is an aspect of him.
- Take your natural symbol to your altar and light the candles. Burn the pine incense if you are using it, to connect with the forest.
- Hold your natural symbol in your hands and repeat the following invocation three times:

I call on Robin, King of the wood,
He who is known as Robin Hood.
Of his strength I do partake
As this magical spell I make.
I weave the power round and round;
Deep within, my courage is found.
Blessed be!

- Keep the natural symbol close to you, perhaps placing it in a spell pouch and wearing it around your neck. This is now your talisman of strength and courage. And remember, all you will ever need is already within you.

Arrow of Truth Spell

This spell will enable you to learn the truth about a chosen situation. If you choose to work it, however, be aware that the truth may not be what you wanted to hear.

Purpose of ritual: to discover the truth of a situation
What you need: a large darning needle, a sheet of paper, a pen, a white candle, a little sunflower oil, some dried basil, your pentacle

- Take all the items to your altar and cast a Circle.
- Place the darning needle on the pentacle, on your altar, to charge.
- On the sheet of paper, write down, in full, the situation you would like to know about. Be as honest as possible and stick to the facts as you know them.
- Take up the needle and say:

This needle now represents Robin's Arrow;
It is the Arrow of Truth. So be it!

- Place the needle back on the pentacle.
- Anoint the white candle with a little sunflower oil and roll it in the dried basil. Place the candle in a sturdy holder.
- Fold up the sheet of paper, making sure that the writing is on the inside, and place it beneath or in front of the candle holder.
- Holding the candle firmly, close your eyes and point out a place on the candle.
- Open your eyes and gently stick the needle – the arrow of truth – into the candle at the point where you touched it.
- Light the candle and allow it to burn until the needle falls out.
- Extinguish the candle and keep the needle safe for future spells. You will have the truth within a moon cycle.

March

Dawn 05.50 Dusk 18.21

Monday 27th			
Moon quarter	4th (waning)	Herb or incense	Catnip
Moon sign	♓	Crystal	Bloodstone
Colour	Red	Sun sign	♈

Tuesday 28th			
Moon quarter	4th (waning)	Herb or incense	Pine
Moon sign	♓ 20.31 ♈	Crystal	Hematite
Colour	Purple	Sun sign	♈

Wednesday 29th			
Moon phase	●	Herb or incense	Jasmine
Time	10.15	Crystal	Obsidian
Moon quarter	1st (waxing)	Sun sign	♈
Moon sign	♈	Special	● Total Eclipse
Colour	Orange		

Thursday 30th			
Moon quarter	1st (waxing)	Herb or incense	Frankincense
Moon sign	♈ 21.01 ♉	Crystal	Moonstone
Colour	Brown	Sun sign	♈

Friday 31st			
Moon quarter	1st (waxing)	Herb or incense	Fennel
Moon sign	♉	Crystal	Amber
Colour	Gold	Sun sign	♈

Financial Growth Pouch

Purpose of ritual: to use the fertile energies of the sabbat to increase finances

What you need: a small green pouch or envelope, patchouli oil, a small silver pentagram (perhaps from an old necklace), a clear quartz crystal, a white feather, a £1 coin, your pentacle

- Place all the items on your pentacle to charge, then spend 10 to 15 minutes chanting the prosperity chant given on page 56.

- Place the pentagram, crystal, feather and coin in the pouch and anoint it with a little patchouli oil. Say this spell three times:

Stone of earth, Coin of mint,
Feather of sky, Symbol of witch,
Enchanted be! Bring wealth to me!
Stone of earth, Coin of mint,
Feather of sky, Symbol of witch,
My wealth will grow. Be it so!

- Place the pouch in your wallet or purse and keep it with you.

Enchanted Pool Scrying

Scrying is the art of seeing the future, in this case in an enchanted pool. Remember that any form of divination takes practice to perfect, so perform this little rite as often as you can, making sure you record your visions and so forth at the end of each session.

Purpose of ritual: to perform a divination
What you need: a pretty glass or crystal bowl; green, blue or turquoise food colouring; a faceted crystal of clear quartz; pebbles and shells; a blue candle; pure spring water

- Place the bowl in the middle of your altar and arrange the pebbles and shells in it. Place the quartz crystal in the centre of these pebbles to form a focal point for scrying.
- Fill the bowl with spring water and enough food colouring to turn the water the colour of an enchanted pool.
- Place the blue candle in a holder at the back of the bowl and light it. Position it so that its flame gently lights the pool but doesn't distract your vision.
- Take three deep breaths and gaze into the depths of the crystal at the centre of the enchanted pool. Focus on a particular question if you like, or just see what images and words flit through your mind. What do you see? What do you hear? What does all this mean to you? If it doesn't make sense to you now, make a note of any words, images, songs or visions, and keep it in your Book of Shadows. You may find at a later date that it all makes perfect sense.

Camelot

Last night I had the strangest dream,
I walked through Camelot, unseen.
Like a ghost I trod the cobbled streets
And saw armoured knights perform great feats.
With a flowing gown and hair of gold,
To Lancelot my heart I sold.
No return of love did he make,
And so I wept beside the lake.
O, Camelot, Camelot, strong and true,
So often have I dreamt of you.

When Arthur was a mighty king,
And maidens to a harp would sing,
When jousting tournaments were held,
And injustice and dishonour quelled,
O Lancelot, my heart you've won;
Courageous knight, what have you done?
For how can I wake in my own land
And leave my soul within your hand?
O, Camelot, Camelot, strong and true,
So often have I dreamt of you.

April

Throughout the coming days we will feel the sun strengthening and see the world open up in a profusion of springtime blooms. The days grow longer and the soft rains of April nourish the Earth, bringing forth her fertile scent. Daisies and buttercups adorn gardens and grassy banks, and bluebells begin to show off their beautiful violet colours.

The tree associated with this month is the hawthorn. In April, the first white flowers are seen on its branches, although it will not blossom fully until next month (hence its country name, May blossom). As mentioned earlier, the hawthorn is part of the faery triad, and it is considered a most magical tree. A ring of mushrooms or toadstools growing around a solitary hawthorn tree is a sure sign of faery activity and may even be a gateway to the Otherworld or Underworld.

The hawthorn was sacred to the ancient Celts, and any Celt found felling one was condemned to death. They called it huathe, and to them it was a tree of protective energy. This may be due largely to its sharp thorns! The protective magic of the hawthorn continues to be invoked in the practice of planting hawthorn hedges as perimeter borders. My own garden has both a hawthorn tree and a hawthorn hedge, and the energies around my home are very protective and positive.

According to tree lore, the hawthorn is a tree of chastity, symbolising the wisdom that at times it is better to keep oneself to oneself. The hawthorn also teaches us to wait patiently – that which we most wish for will come to us in good time, providing it is for our greater good.

In Wiccan belief the hawthorn is known as the goddess tree, because of the mantle of white blossom it wears in spring, and it is especially sacred to the Welsh sun goddess, Olwen.

The flower of April is the daisy, which stands for innocence and freshness, linking it to the Maiden and spring in general. The word daisy is derived from 'day's eye', which refers to the way that the flower follows the path of the sun and then closes at dusk. A daisy chain worn around the head symbolises the Maiden's crown, and is perfect for springtime rituals.

The herbs of this month are patchouli and thyme. These can be burnt as incense in their dried form, or they can be planted with a wish for the growth of a project or plan. As we are still well within the realms of fertility magic throughout the months of April and May, you could mix equal parts of dried patchouli and thyme, and place them in a small pouch, together with a slip of paper on which you have written the project you wish to fertilise and bring to fruition. Sleep with this pouch beneath your pillow for three nights and then empty the contents into the earth, asking for the blessing of success. In my own magical endeavours, I always associate the month of April with the deity aspects of King Arthur and his queen Gueniever. You will probably be familiar with the Arthurian legends, the tales of the great sword Excalibur and the Knights of the Round Table. As I have loved these tales since early childhood, I was thrilled to learn during my early days in the Craft that King Arthur and his queen are actually just another aspect of the witches' God and Goddess and that I could call on their energies and attune with them in ritual. Indeed, many Pagans, particularly those dedicated to the Celtic pantheon, choose to work with these deities all the time.

The spells and rituals for this month will mostly relate to the Arthurian legends. These are among the first spells I performed.

To Summon a Lover

For this ritual you will need to find a secluded outdoor space where a hawthorn grows. It is best if you can walk around the hawthorn, but if that isn't possible, perform the ritual in front of the tree.

Purpose of ritual: to bring a new love into your life
What you need: two red roses, a red or pink chiffon scarf (or a drum), 50 cm/20 in of red ribbon, scissors, your chalice, some red wine or grape juice, a CD player and a CD of soft music (optional)

- Lay your tools on the grass and cast a Circle, ensuring that the hawthorn tree is within the magical boundary.
- Place the roses in the middle of the Circle to form an equal-armed cross. Cut a small lock from your hair, tie it to the red ribbon, and lay it next to the roses. Pour some wine or juice into the chalice.
- Begin to move around the circle, deosil, in a slow, seductive dance. Hum or sing if you feel like it, or play the CD. As you dance, wave patterns with the scarf or beat the drum. Concentrate your energies on attuning with the Goddess tree and summoning the lover you require.
- Once you feel connected to the land, the tree and the power, begin to chant this spell, and continue as long as you remain focused:

By earth, by wind, by land, by sea,
I summon a lover to come to me.
By witch's dance and Goddess tree,
I summon a lover to come to me.
By earth, by wind, by land, by sea,
I summon a lover to come to me.
By power raised I send my plea;
I summon a lover to come to me.

- When you have finished chanting, tie the ribbon and lock of hair to the hawthorn tree, asking for the fruition of your spell.
- Pour a little of the red wine or grape juice at the foot of the tree, tap your chalice against the tree trunk and say:

Blessed Be!

- Drink the rest of the wine or juice from your chalice and, finally, leave a single red rose at the foot of the tree in thanks. Take the other one home with you to place on your altar.

April

Dawn 05.50
Dusk 18.21

Saturday 1st			
Moon quarter	1st (waxing)	Herb or incense	Lavender
Moon sign	♉ 23.49 ♊	Crystal	Kunzite
Colour	Black	Sun sign	♈
		Special	All Fools' Day

Sunday 2nd			
Moon quarter	1st (waxing)	Herb or incense	Jasmine
Moon sign	♊	Crystal	Topaz
Colour	Green	Sun sign	♈

Arthurian Triple Goddess Rite

The Triple Goddess of Arthurian legend is made up as follows. Elaine, the lily maid of Astolat, takes the role of the Maiden. Queen Gueniever takes the role of the Mother, and, of course, Morgan Le Fey plays the part of the Crone/Dark Goddess. Remember that 'dark' does not necessarily mean evil; it can simply refer, as in this case, to the hidden mysteries.

Purpose of ritual: to attune with the Celtic Triple Goddess

What you need: three pillar candles (red, white and black); essential oils of lily of the valley, rosemary and cedarwood; three small paint brushes; a poster, picture, book or other object that represents the Arthurian realm (alternatively, try using a CD of new age music)

- Take everything you need to your altar. Display the picture, book or object that represents the Arthurian realm, or put the music on softly in the background.

- Take up the white candle, and, using a paint brush, anoint it with lily of the valley essential oil. When it is evenly scented, place it on the altar at the 12 o'clock position. This is the Maiden candle. It represents Elaine, who was the guardian of Lancelot's shield, and who eventually fell in love with the great knight. She can help you with problems of unrequited love as well as with more traditional Maiden aspects of magic.

- Light the Maiden candle and say:

*I name this candle for Elaine, the fair lily maid of Astolat.
May she bless me with her love.*

- Now move on to the red candle and anoint it with the rosemary oil. This is the Mother candle and it represents Gueniever, Queen of all Camelot. Powerful, beautiful, generous and with the courage of her convictions (remember how she behaved with regard to Lancelot) she can help you to be true to yourself.

- Light the Mother candle, place it at 8 o'clock on your altar and say:

I name this candle for Gueniever, Queen to Camelot, wife to Arthur, lover to Lancelot, true to herself. May she shower me with her gifts.

- Finally, take up the black candle and anoint it with the oil of cedarwood. Place it at the 4 o'clock position on your altar. (All three candles should now form a triangle.) The black candle represents the Dark Goddess and Crone, Morgan Le Fey, enchantress and sorcerer.

- Light the Crone candle and say:

I name this candle for Morgan Le Fey, weaver of magic and spells, keeper of mysteries. May she bless me with her magical knowledge.

- Allow the candles to burn for as long as you are with them, letting their fine fragrances mingle. Then extinguish them and keep them to commune with the Arthurian Triple Goddess. (Don't use them for any other purpose.)

April

Dawn 05.36
Dusk 18.33

Monday 3rd			
Moon quarter	1st (waxing)	Herb or incense	Catnip
Moon sign	♊	Crystal	Amber
Colour	Pink	Sun sign	♈

Tuesday 4th			
Moon quarter	1st (waxing)	Herb or incense	Valerian
Moon sign	♊ 06.15 ♋	Crystal	Jasper
Colour	Orange	Sun sign	♈

Wednesday 5th			
Moon phase	◐	Colour	White
Time	12.01	Herb or incense	Bay
Moon quarter	2nd (waxing)	Crystal	Aventurine
Moon sign	♋	Sun sign	♈

Thursday 6th			
Moon quarter	2nd (waxing)	Crystal	Rose Quartz
Moon sign	♋ 16.25 ♌	Sun sign	♈
Colour	Silver	Special	01.21 Venus ♀ enters Pisces ♓
Herb or incense	Angelica		

Friday 7th			
Moon quarter	2nd (waxing)	Herb or incense	Mint
Moon sign	♌	Crystal	Tiger's Eye
Colour	Brown	Sun sign	♈

Saturday 8th			
Moon quarter	2nd (waxing)	Herb or incense	Mace
Moon sign	♌	Crystal	Hematite
Colour	Gold	Sun sign	♈

Sunday 9th			
Moon quarter	2nd (waxing)	Herb or incense	Ginger
Moon sign	♌ 04.48 ♍	Crystal	Obsidian
Colour	Purple	Sun sign	♈

Witches' God Candle Rite

In this ritual we use a gold candle because King Arthur is a sun god.

Purpose of ritual: to attune with the energies of King Arthur
What you need: a large gold pillar candle, some sunflower oil, some dried sunflower petals or sunflower seeds

- Take the items to your altar or, if you prefer, to a sacred space outdoors.
- Anoint the pillar candle with the sunflower oil and then set it in the middle of your altar. Surround it with a circle of sunflower petals or sunflower seeds.
- Light the candle and say the following words three times:

I call on Arthur, warrior king;
I welcome the gifts that he may bring.
Farewell winter, welcome spring.
Rejoice within the magical ring.
Hero of battle, hero of love,
Shining the light down from above,
Wielder of sword, wielder of power,
I welcome now the Sun God's hour.

- Commune with Arthur in meditation as the God candle burns.
- Once you have completed your rite, extinguish the candle and keep it for future meditations on Arthur. Scatter the petals or seeds outdoors.

April

Dawn 05.20 Dusk 18.43

Monday 10th

Moon quarter	2nd (waxing)	Herb or incense	Parsley
Moon sign	♍	Crystal	Sodalite
Colour	Yellow	Sun sign	♈

Tuesday 11th

Moon quarter	2nd (waxing)	Herb or incense	Cinnamon
Moon sign	♍ 17.47 ♎	Crystal	Carnelian
Colour	Silver	Sun sign	♈

Wednesday 12th

Moon quarter	2nd (waxing)	Herb or incense	Thyme
Moon sign	♎	Crystal	Moonstone
Colour	Grey	Sun sign	♈

Thursday 13th

Moon phase	○	Crystal	Snowflake-Obsidian
Time	16.40	Sun sign	♈
Moon quarter	3rd (waning)	Special	Seed Moon
Moon sign	♎		First confession of witchcraft (without torture) by Isobel Gowdie in Scotland 1662
Colour	Jade		
Herb or incense	Pine		

Friday 14th

Moon quarter	3rd (waning)	Crystal	Jasper
Moon sign	♎ 05.08 ♏	Sun sign	♈
Colour	Orange	Special	00.59 Mars ♂ enters Cancer ♋
Herb or incense	Mugwort		

Saturday 15th

Moon quarter	3rd (waning)	Herb or incense	Catnip
Moon sign	♏	Crystal	Bloodstone
Colour	Blue	Sun sign	♈

Sunday 16th

Moon quarter	3rd (waning)	Crystal	Citrine
Moon sign	♏ 14.19 ♐	Sun sign	♈
Colour	Purple	Special	Easter Day
Herb or incense	Borage		12.20 Mercury ☿ enters Aries ♈

SEED MOON

The full moon of April is traditionally known as the seed moon, so it is an excellent time to plant a herb garden for your magic.

You could also use this time to commune with Gueniever, the Mother aspect of this month's Goddess.

To Name a Sword

As I mentioned earlier, a sword can make an excellent ritual tool, either as a substitute for an athame, or in addition to one.

Swords have a wonderful aura of magic about them. All great heroes of myth and legend have an equally famous sword. King Arthur had Excalibur; Robin of Sherwood had Albion, one of the seven swords of Wayland; and, in fiction, Aragorn (from *The Lord of the Rings*) had Anduril. In Norse mythology, it was believed that a Viking warrior must die with his sword in his hand if he was to spend his eternal life in Valhalla – the Norse Otherworld.

By far the most impressive sword I have ever seen belonged not to a hero of legend, but to the great historical warrior William Wallace. Known as the Wallace Sword, or the Sword of Freedom, this massive weapon is one of Scotland's national treasures. It is kept safely within the Wallace National Monument in Stirling, and is so huge it has to be seen to be believed! If you ever get a chance to go and see this fabulous sword, which simply oozes the magic of history and courage, it's well worth the long climb up the spiral staircase – the view from the top of the tower's not bad either!

For ritual, though, a small blade can be bought from occult stores, from some new age stores and via the internet. Pick a sword with a scabbard to protect the blade when it's not in use. And take the weight of the sword into consideration – you want one that's light enough to cast a Circle with comfortably.

Once you have your sword, you need to think of a sacred name. Swords are forged in fire, so any name that includes this element would be appropriate. Does the sword make a sound as it moves through the air? Does it have jewels or stones on the hilt? Take your time when choosing a name. The right one will come to you if you are patient. If you are having real difficulty, here are a few suggestions to get you going: Firedrake, Spellsinger, Flame-dancer, Lady Knight, Star-striker, Web-weaver, Storm Tamer ... and so on.

Purpose of ritual: to give a ritual sword a sacred name
What you need: your sword, a scabbard if you have one, sea salt, water, your chalice, your athame or wand, a stick of your favourite incense

- Take your sword to your altar, light the illuminator candles and cast the Circle in the usual way.
- Pour the water into your chalice and add three pinches of sea salt. Stir the mixture three times deosil with your athame or wand.
- Lay the sword across your knee, removing the scabbard if it has one. Light the incense stick and pass it all around the sword, watching as the smokes curls around the blade and the hilt. Say:

I cleanse and consecrate this sword, in the name of the Lord and Lady. Blessed be!

- Do the same thing with the scabbard.
- Sprinkle the blade and hilt of the sword with the water and say:

I name this sword -------.
May it be true to my power as a witch.
It is now a sacred ritual tool. Blessed be!

- Once again, repeat this procedure with the scabbard. Your sword is now ready to use in ritual.

SUN MOVES INTO TAURUS

The sun enters Taurus, the sign of the bull, on May 20th. The ruling planet of Taurus is Venus, the planet of love and an aspect of the Mother Goddess. This can make Taureans quite nurturing and affectionate. The power stone for Taurus is the diamond, and the birth stone is the emerald, so both these stones could be incorporated into magical spells or worn as talismans.

Taureans can sometimes become self-absorbed and give in to a victim mentality, going through a 'woe is me!' period. This can make those around them impatient and may leave Taurus wondering why they are so lonely! However, at their best Taureans are loving, loyal, affectionate and very generous. They have a creative side and are extremely sociable, loving nothing more than a good party.

April

Dawn 05.05
Dusk 18.54

Monday 17th

Moon quarter	3rd (waning)	Herb or incense	Cinnamon
Moon sign	♐	Crystal	Amethyst
Colour	Grey	Sun sign	♈

Tuesday 18th

Moon quarter	3rd (waning)	Herb or incense	Mint
Moon sign	♐ 21.13 ♑	Crystal	Jasper
Colour	Yellow	Sun sign	♈

Wednesday 19th

Moon quarter	3rd (waning)	Herb or incense	Sage
Moon sign	♑	Crystal	Smokey Quartz
Colour	Indigo	Sun sign	♈

Thursday 20th

Moon quarter	3rd (waning)	Herb or incense	Dill
Moon sign	♑	Crystal	Moonstone
Colour	Peach	Sun sign	♈ 05.26 ♉

Friday 21st

Moon phase	◑	Colour	Blue
Time	03.28	Herb or incense	Parsley
Moon quarter	4th (waning)	Crystal	Aventurine
Moon sign	♑ 01.56 ♒	Sun sign	♉

Saturday 22nd

Moon quarter	4th (waning)	Crystal	Citrine
Moon sign	♒	Sun sign	♉
Colour	Pink	Special	Earth Day
Herb or incense	Borage		

Sunday 23rd

Moon quarter	4th (waning)	Herb or incense	Fennel
Moon sign	♒ 04.43 ♓	Crystal	Bloodstone
Colour	Green	Sun sign	♉

Making a Magical Staff

When I think of great wizards such as the legendary Merlin and the fictional Gandalf, I always think of the magical staff. The staff is really a larger version of the wand, and it can be used to cast Circles and direct power in the same way as a wand, athame or sword. It can also be stood across a doorway as a form of protection.

My friend Jenny has a large black staff topped with a silver dragon. She's very into dragon magic, so this ritual tool is perfect for her, and as she lives in a mountainous region of Tennessee, USA, it also comes in handy to lean on when she goes walking in nature!

Although staffs are available to buy, they can be expensive and you can easily make your own. All you need is a sturdy piece of wood that reaches from the floor to your shoulder in height. This should be rounded at one end so that it is comfortable to hold. You can decorate it in whatever way you wish. You might paint it or varnish it, or carve it with runes, your magical name or some Celtic knotwork. You might like to fix something decorative to the top of the staff, maybe a representation of your totem animal or star sign, or perhaps a crystal ball. It's a good idea to wind leather or some form of material around the handle part of the staff to make a grip. Finally, you can wind ribbon or a leather thong around it, from which you can hang feathers, beads, tiny bells (the ones on cat collars are ideal) and magical charms. Use your imagination.

Make your staff personal to you and your magical path. Take your time, and when it's finished, cleanse and consecrate it as you did with the sword, dedicating it to your magic as a ritual tool.

BELTANE EVE

The sabbat Beltane officially starts at sunset on April 30th. Although celebrations don't get into full swing until May 1st, most witches acknowledge May's Eve in some way. A nice tradition is to take equal lengths of white and silver ribbons and tie them in a bow around one of the lower branches of a tree, preferably a hawthorn. Do this at sunset, making a wish and asking the Goddess for her blessings.

April

Dawn 04.52
Dusk 19.06

Monday 24th			
Moon quarter	4th (waning)	Herb or incense	Angelica
Moon sign	♓	Crystal	Topaz
Colour	Purple	Sun sign	♉

Tuesday 25th			
Moon quarter	4th (waning)	Herb or incense	Catnip
Moon sign	♓ 06.12 ♈	Crystal	Tiger's Eye
Colour	Jade	Sun sign	♉

Wednesday 26th			
Moon quarter	4th (waning)	Herb or incense	Mugwort
Moon sign	♈	Crystal	Jasper
Colour	White	Sun sign	♉

Thursday 27th			
Moon phase	●	Colour	Brown
Time	19.44	Herb or incense	Bayberry
Moon quarter	1st (waxing)	Crystal	Hematite
Moon sign	♈ 07.27 ♉	Sun sign	♉

Friday 28th			
Moon quarter	1st (waxing)	Herb or incense	Mint
Moon sign	♉	Crystal	Rose Quartz
Colour	Indigo	Sun sign	♉

Saturday 29th			
Moon quarter	1st (waxing)	Herb or incense	Catnip
Moon sign	♉ 09.58 ♊	Crystal	Snowy Quartz
Colour	White	Sun sign	♉

Sunday 30th			
Moon quarter	1st (waxing)	Crystal	Carnelian
Moon sign	♊	Sun sign	♉
Colour	Red	Special	May's Eve
Herb or incense	Valerian		Beltane begins

The Knight in Me

I strive to find the knight in me;
I know he's there inside,
For when my way I cannot see,
I do not run and hide.

I go my own way fearlessly,
Face each problem as it arrives;
I stand my ground, I do not flee;
That way, I know I'll survive.

If you run from your foe, he will chase you;
Don't beg for mercy and lose all your pride.
To your heart you must remain true
And look for the knight inside.

So I strive to find the knight in me;
I know he's there somewhere,
And I hope of his courage and valour
He will give me one small share.

May

May is a month of magic, which begins with the festival of Beltane and continues with parades, parties, may-poles and morris dancing. The warm sun filters through newly clothed trees, the birds sing and call to each other after their long winter silence and the bluebell woods are a vision of violet. Spring is definitely here and summer is only a breath away.

This month's sacred tree is the oak, known as duir to the ancient Celts, to whom it represented great strength, survival and the power to overcome the challenges placed before us. This is the third and final tree of the faery triad, revered not only by the Celts but also by the Druids. The Vikings held this tree sacred to Thor, as it is often struck by lightning!

Most people are acquainted with the strength of the oak, for it was used historically in ship-building and to make strong foundations and thick doors for medieval castles. Due to this strength and to its majesty, the oak is known as King of the Woods. In magical terms, the oak tree is a door between worlds, and many divination tools are crafted from its wood in order to make the art of 'seeing' easier. The oak will forever represent all that is best about traditional England, conjuring up images of Robin Hood and Herne the Hunter. The true spirit of the oak is one of determination, strength, leadership and steadfastness.

In contrast to the mighty oak, the flower associated with the month of May is the gentle, fragrant lilac. In the language of flowers the lilac stands for first love, in the sense both of romantic love and of the awakening of the natural world to the call of spring and fertility. Everywhere creatures are finding partners and dancing to the tune of the creation of life.

The herbs of May are lavender and parsley, so you could include parsley in your May feasts or maybe create a lavender-filled sleep pillow – add a little mugwort too if you wish to enjoy prophetic dreams.

Goddess Blessing

Most witches perform some kind of daily acknowledgement of all the good things in their lives. We see these things as blessings from the Goddess, and so we commune with her for a few moments each day in a simple meditation or prayer in order to bless her in our turn. By doing this, we are constantly acknowledging all that we have – which is the best way to make sure that it continues, as to express gratitude for abundance is also to ask for it.

Many people like to perform a Goddess blessing first thing in the morning as it gears them up for the day ahead. Personally, I prefer to perform the blessing in the evening, making it a quiet reflective time at the end of the day. Do whatever suits you best.

A Goddess blessing is a very personal thing, and you may feel that you would like to create your own. In fact, you will find in general that as you move deeper into the Craft, you will rely less and less on the rituals and spells of other witches, prefering to devise your own. The first successful ritual you create will become something of a cornerstone in your magical work and will stand as testimony to how far you have come down the magical path. If you feel ready for this stage right now, that's great. If not, don't worry. You'll get there in your own time. If you don't want to create your own ritual, you might like to write your own words for the blessing. Alternatively, you can use the words given here. If the idea of talking to a goddess doesn't appeal to you, then simply reword the ritual, substituting your chosen divinity, or maybe just 'the powers that be'.

Purpose of ritual: to express thanks for the blessings of the Goddess
What you need: background music – for example, meditation music, nature sounds or music specially written for use in magic (optional); an incense or essential oil of your choice – for example Night Queen incense, which will carry your messages straight to the Goddess (optional)

- All formal blessings take place at the altar, so make sure that your altar is clean and that any flowers you have there are fresh and free from dead heads.

- If you are using music, start it playing softly, and if applicable light your incense or oil burner. Light the illuminator candles and settle down before your altar.

- Take a few calming breaths and clear your mind. When your breath is steady and you feel ready, speak these (or your own) words to the Lady, focusing on her light and unconditional love:

Gentle Lady, Mother of All, I come here in honour and in thanks. Thank you for all the wonderful things in my life right now and for all the lovely things that are coming to me. Thank you for all the success I have enjoyed so far and for all the successes that are to come. Thank you for all the love and friendship I give and receive, and for the protection you offer me and my family. I honour your divine presence in the natural world around me. May you continue to shower me with your gifts of love and abundance. So mote it be!

- If you like you can extinguish the candles and go about your day, or you might like to commune with the divinity for a little longer.

BELTANE

On May 1st the festival of Beltane really gets under way. Beltane is a major fertility sabbat, at which witches work magically towards the success of plans and projects, the achievement of goals, the prosperity of businesses and, of course, the conception and birth of healthy children and animals.

Beltane is not about orgies and sexual depravity – so if you go to a festival in search of these things you will be sadly disappointed! It is simply a welcoming of spring and summer and all the wonderful gifts nature gives us. It also begins the season of faery magic, and the Faery Queen (an aspect of the Goddess – well, I did tell you she had many faces!) is represented by the Queen of the May in May Day celebrations and parades.

Another ancient Pagan tradition that continues today is the dancing of the maypole. The woven maypole ribbons are symbolic of the web of life, while the maypole itself represents the God, and the wreath of flowers placed around the top of the pole represents the Goddess.

Beltane is also a fire festival, and our ancestors would celebrate it by lighting a bonfire, commonly termed a balefire or belfire. The balefire takes its name from the Celtic sun god Bel, and in ancient times sacrifices were offered up to him around it. In farming communities two balefires were lit and livestock were driven between them in a symbolic cleansing. It was hoped that these animals would then be blessed and protected from all harm, but one can only imagine the fear and discomfort the poor animals felt while being driven so close to two roaring fires.

The colours of Beltane are red and white, and you should decorate your altar accordingly with red and white candles, ribbons and flowers. Wreaths and garlands of ivy can be used too, as can vases of lilac, May blossom and bluebells. Traditional Beltane fragrances are lilac and lavender, and you might like to include a touch of ylang-ylang. On your altar you should place a representation of a springtime goddess, or maybe a fairy or dryad. As this is also a time when the masculine energy of nature is strongly felt, you should place a statue or picture of the God on or near your altar. I personally feel that a figure of Pan is particularly appropriate. He has a wonderful mischievous spirit and is renowned as a fertility god! Alternatively, you may prefer the energies of Robin Hood, King Arthur, Herne the Hunter, Apollo or Helios.

Pan pipe music could provide the background to your Beltane ritual, or you could use a CD of nature sounds. Your feast should include fruits, lemon cake, Madeira cake and elderberry wine. On a recent trip to Scotland I bought a bottle of spring oak leaf wine, which tasted lovely and is very appropriate for this ritual. Look around and you may be able to find something similar in your own area. If you live in Scotland, lucky you! You have the whole range of oak leaf wines, bramble wines and heather liqueurs at your disposal!

Any of the spells in this chapter could be used as a part of your Beltane celebrations. And don't forget to make the most of the public festivities on offer – chances are there will be like-minded people there for you to meet and chat with. Wear your pentacle with pride, and – most of all – have fun! Enjoy the sabbat, that's part of what witchcraft is all about.

May

Dawn 04.38
Dusk 19.16

Monday 1st

Moon quarter	1st (waxing)	Crystal	Clear Quartz
Moon sign	♊ 15.17 ♋	Sun sign	♉
Colour	White	Special	Beltane
Herb or incense	Lavender		

Tuesday 2nd

Moon quarter	1st (waxing)	Herb or incense	Pine
Moon sign	♋	Crystal	Kunzite
Colour	Green	Sun sign	♉

Wednesday 3rd

Moon quarter	1st (waxing)	Crystal	Amethyst
Moon sign	♋	Sun sign	♉
Colour	Purple	Special	10.25 Venus ♀
Herb or incense	Fennel		enters Aries ♈

Thursday 4th

Moon quarter	1st (waxing)	Herb or incense	Jasmine
Moon sign	♋ 00.18 ♌	Crystal	Sodalite
Colour	Yellow	Sun sign	♉

Friday 5th

Moon phase	◐	Herb or incense	Catnip
Time	05.13	Crystal	Aventurine
Moon quarter	2nd (waxing)	Sun sign	♉
Moon sign	♌	Special	08.28 Mercury ☿
Colour	White		enters Taurus ♉

Saturday 6th

Moon quarter	2nd (waxing)	Herb or incense	Ginger
Moon sign	♌ 12.20 ♍	Crystal	Topaz
Colour	Gold	Sun sign	♉

Sunday 7th

Moon quarter	2nd (waxing)	Herb or incense	Sage
Moon sign	♍	Crystal	Amber
Colour	Pink	Sun sign	♉

Scrying the Clouds

Scrying is the term given to the art of 'seeing' or fortune-telling. It is a form of divination and can be performed using one of several natural tools, such as a pool of water, fire, crystals, rain or, as in this case, the clouds. Scrying the clouds is one of the most effective ways to relax, and children practise this game quite naturally.

All you need is a blanket or rug to lie on and a clear view of the sky. If you want an answer to a particular question or problem that you are currently facing, then lie back, focus on the issue at hand and close your eyes. If you don't have a current dilemma (lucky you!) then simply clear your mind and focus on your wish for guidance.

Once you are nicely relaxed, open your eyes and scan the clouds above you. Look for patterns and pictures and interpret them using your intuition. Here are a few pointers: a wall or maze may mean that there are blocks on your current path; boats, cars, trains and so on could indicate a holiday or journey of some sort; a tree might represent strength; a human shape could indicate a loved one or a stranger; a book or desk could indicate knowledge or a course of study; and flowers, hearts, birds and angel shapes might all be good omens.

Don't forget to take note of the colour and density of the clouds. If a particular shape appears within thick, dark grey clouds, this probably means there are obstacles surrounding the issue that this shape represents. If, however, the same shape appears within wispy, white, fluffy clouds, this may be an indication that any blocks will soon be cleared and you will be free to move forwards.

Do take into account your own individuality – the same shape may provoke different responses from different people. For example, you might see a large cloud shaped like a spider and feel really happy about that. You take it as a positive sign, as the spider is one of your totem creatures. However, should I see the very same cloud I'd be up and running so fast even a thing with eight legs couldn't keep up! For me the spider would be either a negative sign, or an indication that I should face my fears. So use your instinct while scrying, and keep a written record of what you see and how you interpret it.

Faery Ring

May is the first of the months associated with strong workings of faery magic. The faeries, or fey, as they are also called, are the devic spirits of nature. They reside in rocks, trees, flowers, meadows and so on. Another name for the faeries is elementals – you should use whichever term you feel most comfortable with.

Purpose of ritual: to ask the faeries for assistance with a problem
What you need: a packet of wild flower seeds, a saucer of milk or honey as an offering.

- Go out into nature and find a secluded and wild spot.
- Sit for a few minutes taking in the scene around you and try to sense any faery activity. Ponder the matter you require elemental assistance with, and if you like tell the fey all about it. You can do this either verbally or in your head, it doesn't matter – the faeries will hear you.
- With your wild flower seeds begin to cast a Circle, by scattering them as you move deosil in a circle. This is now a faery ring.
- Place your offering of milk or honey in the centre of the magical ring.
- Continue to ponder your current challenge, asking the fey for help. You may like to chant these words or similar:

  Earth, wind, water, fire,
  Faery power, bring my desire.

- When you feel that your request has been heard, return home, leaving the offering and the faery ring behind. Know that you can return to this sacred spot whenever you require faery assistance with something – but don't forget to leave an offering in return.

HARE MOON

The full moon of May is traditionally called the hare moon, so this esbat is an excellent time to attune with this magical creature.

May

Dawn 04.26
Dusk 19.27

Monday 8th

Moon quarter	2nd (waxing)	Herb or incense	Dill
Moon sign	♍	Crystal	Jasper
Colour	Black	Sun sign	♉

Tuesday 9th

Moon quarter	2nd (waxing)	Herb or incense	Mace
Moon sign	♍ 01.10 ♎	Crystal	Tiger's Eye
Colour	Green	Sun sign	♉

Wednesday 10th

Moon quarter	2nd (waxing)	Herb or incense	Angelica
Moon sign	♎	Crystal	Carnelian
Colour	Brown	Sun sign	♉

Thursday 11th

Moon quarter	2nd (waxing)	Herb or incense	Cinnamon
Moon sign	♎ 12.25 ♏	Crystal	Rose Quartz
Colour	Orange	Sun sign	♉

Friday 12th

Moon quarter	2nd (waxing)	Herb or incense	Rosemary
Moon sign	♏	Crystal	Snowy Quartz
Colour	Red	Sun sign	♉

Saturday 13th

Moon phase	○	Herb or incense	Jasmine
Time	06.51	Crystal	Moonstone
Moon quarter	3rd (waning)	Sun sign	♉
Moon sign	♏ 20.56 ♐	Special	Hare Moon
Colour	Silver		

Sunday 14th

Moon quarter	3rd (waning)	Herb or incense	Mace
Moon sign	♐	Crystal	Smokey Quartz
Colour	Grey	Sun sign	♉

May

Dawn 04.16
Dusk 19.37

Monday 15th			
Moon quarter	3rd (waning)	Herb or incense	Bay
Moon sign	♐	Crystal	Hematite
Colour	Blue	Sun sign	♉

Tuesday 16th			
Moon quarter	3rd (waning)	Herb or incense	Dill
Moon sign	♐ 02.59 ♑	Crystal	Moonstone
Colour	Indigo	Sun sign	♉

Wednesday 17th			
Moon quarter	3rd (waning)	Herb or incense	Parsley
Moon sign	♑	Crystal	Citrine
Colour	Gold	Sun sign	♉

Thursday 18th			
Moon quarter	3rd (waning)	Herb or incense	Sage
Moon sign	♑ 07.19 ♒	Crystal	Bloodstone
Colour	White	Sun sign	♉

Friday 19th			
Moon quarter	3rd (waning)	Crystal	Snowflake-Obsidian
Moon sign	♒	Sun sign	♉
Colour	Green	Special	20.52 Mercury ☿
Herb or incense	Thyme		enters Gemini ♊

Saturday 20th			
Moon phase	◑	Colour	Red
Time	09.21	Herb or incense	Bay
Moon quarter	4th (waning)	Crystal	Moonstone
Moon sign	♒ 10.39 ♓	Sun sign	♉

Sunday 21st			
Moon quarter	4th (waning)	Herb or incense	Fennel
Moon sign	♓	Crystal	Kunzite
Colour	Peach	Sun sign	♉ 04.32 ♊

SUN MOVES INTO GEMINI

May 21st is the first day of Gemini, the sign of the twins. Its power stone is citrine and its birth stone is the beautiful diamond. The ruling planet is Mercury. In mythology, Mercury was the messenger between the gods and men. He is depicted wearing a winged helmet and has wings at his ankles, enabling him to deliver messages speedily. It is due to this swiftness that he was also adopted as the god of thieves!

The most common complaint against Geminis is that they appear to have a dual personality. One moment they are moody and sullen and the next they are all sweetness and light. This is largely due to the fact that the sign of Gemini embodies the spirit of both light and dark within it. This can make those born under this sign subject to natural emotional highs and lows. A Gemini can be impatient, and they keep their emotions firmly under wraps. They are extremely sociable, often to the point of excluding their loved ones in favour of a series of party nights! At their best, Geminis are naturally inquisitive, adaptable and perceptive.

Craft Devotional

In addition to spending a few moments each day on a Goddess blessing (see pages 112–13), you might also like to perform a Craft devotional, re-affirming your commitment to a positive and magical way of living. If you wish, you can add the Craft devotional to your daily Goddess blessing time. The devotional should be performed at your altar, as it is a formal ritual. Go through the same preparations as for the Goddess blessing, lighting incense, candles and so on. Then clear your mind of mundane chatter, breathe deeply and say these words or ones of your own choosing:

May my feet always walk the path that is right for me. May my heart always be true to myself and considerate of others. May strength and courage always find me when facing adversity. May my lips speak only gentle words of truth. May my eyes be ready to see the good in others and the beauty of nature. May I always have the wisdom to work magic responsibly. May I freely share words of love with those who mean the most to me. And may I always have the vision to see the Goddess and the God as I know them. So be it!

Simply repeating these words at your altar will help you to steer away from any doubts or negative thought patterns. It is also a gentle way to calm feelings of anger or resentment.

May

Dawn 04.06
Dusk 19.46

Monday 22nd			
Moon quarter	4th (waning)	Herb or incense	Borage
Moon sign	♓ 13.24 ♈	Crystal	Bloodstone
Colour	Grey	Sun sign	♊

Tuesday 23rd			
Moon quarter	4th (waning)	Herb or incense	Angelica
Moon sign	♈	Crystal	Hematite
Colour	Jade	Sun sign	♊

Wednesday 24th			
Moon quarter	4th (waning)	Herb or incense	Bayberry
Moon sign	♈ 16.00 ♉	Crystal	Jasper
Colour	Yellow	Sun sign	♊

Thursday 25th			
Moon quarter	4th (waning)	Herb or incense	Jasmine
Moon sign	♉	Crystal	Obsidian
Colour	Brown	Sun sign	♊

Friday 26th			
Moon quarter	4th (waning)	Herb or incense	Pine
Moon sign	♉ 19.19 ♊	Crystal	Sodalite
Colour	White	Sun sign	♊

Saturday 27th			
Moon phase	●	Colour	Blue
Time	05.26	Herb or incense	Mugwort
Moon quarter	1st (waxing)	Crystal	Carnelian
Moon sign	♊	Sun sign	♊

Sunday 28th			
Moon quarter	1st (waxing)	Herb or incense	Nutmeg
Moon sign	♊	Crystal	Aventurine
Colour	Purple	Sun sign	♊

Dawn 03.59 Dusk 19.55

Monday 29th			
Moon quarter	1st (waxing)	Crystal	Citrine
Moon sign	♊ 00.34 ♋	Sun sign	♊
Colour	Green	Special	12.41 Venus ♀ enters Taurus ♉
Herb or incense	Mace		

Tuesday 30th			
Moon quarter	1st (waxing)	Crystal	Rose Quartz
Moon sign	♋	Sun sign	♊
Colour	Indigo	Special	Death of Joan of Arc 1431
Herb or incense	Ginger		

Wednesday 31st			
Moon quarter	1st (waxing)	Herb or incense	Fennel
Moon sign	♋ 08.51 ♌	Crystal	Kunzite
Colour	Grey	Sun sign	♊

Great Holiday Spell

This spell will help to make sure your summer holiday is all that you want it to be.

Purpose of ritual: to ensure your summer break is magical
What you need: a picture of your destination (or its name written on a slip of paper), your pentacle, some incense to represent your destination

- Take the picture of your holiday destination or the slip of paper to your altar. This is now a magical representation of your holiday.
- Place your pentacle in the middle of the altar and light the illuminator candles and the incense.
- Place the picture or slip of paper on your pentacle and hold your hands over it, palms down. Envision a bright white light radiating from your hands into the picture. Focus this magical energy on all the good things you want for your coming holiday.
- Continue for as long as your focus is strong and repeat daily for at least two weeks prior to your holiday.

The Mother

I am the Mother;
I am the moon;
All creatures on Earth respond to my croon.
I am the Goddess;
I am the love;
I am the silver light from above.
Stay in my arms;
Feel my loving embrace;
I nurture your power and fill you with grace.
Mine is the hand that helps infants to walk;
Mine is the voice as they learn how to talk.
Mine is the harvest,
The fruits of my womb;
I weave abundance at the magical loom.
Mine is the gift
Of protection and birth;
Mine is the power that now holds the Earth.

June

June is the month of the summer solstice, when the sun is at its strongest. Our gardens are full of blooms, and their fragrance pervades the air. The song of birds and the gentle hum of bumble bees fills our ears, while butterflies and dragonflies flutter by in a blaze of shimmering, iridescent colour. Summer is a time for work and play, when all creatures make the most of the longer, warmer, brighter days.

In Celtic lore, June is the month of the holly (tinne), which at first seems to be totally out of keeping with the season. Surely the holly tree is associated with winter and the darker months? This is true, and not inconsistent when you know that the association derives from the old folk story of the battle between the Holly King and the Oak King. This is a tale of the seasons, in which the light half of the year, represented by the Oak King, and the dark half, represented by the Holly King, wage war against each other in a bid for supremacy. This battle takes place twice every year, at the summer and winter solstices. In winter, at Yuletide, the Oak King wins the fight, and so the days grow longer and warmer. In summer, the Holly King is victorious, and he sets about bringing us the dark half of the year. In many Pagan circles this battle is acted out as a part of the solstice rituals.

Due to this myth, the holly tree is symbolic of being 'best in fight', and it was once believed that to carry a sprig of holly into battle would bring victory. Carry holly with you if you face animosity or adversity. It has protective qualities and is effective in protection rituals. To guard your home, plant a holly bush at either side of your door.

The flower of June is the rose. Symbolic of feminine beauty, the rose epitomises the gentle, fragrant spirit of summer. As the flower of love, the rose is the first choice for wedding bouquets. Try to pick the most fragrant and incorporate rose oils and incenses into your summer rituals. The herbs associated with the month of June are eucalyptus and lemon balm. These can be dried and burnt as incense or used in spells.

June

Dawn 03.54
Dusk 20.03

Thursday 1st			
Moon quarter	1st (waxing)	Herb or incense	Dill
Moon sign	♌	Crystal	Clear Quartz
Colour	Jade	Sun sign	♊

Friday 2nd			
Moon quarter	1st (waxing)	Herb or incense	Valerian
Moon sign	♌ 20.17 ♍	Crystal	Bloodstone
Colour	Yellow	Sun sign	♊

Saturday 3rd			
Moon phase	◐	Crystal	Opal
Time	23.06	Sun sign	♊
Moon quarter	2nd (waxing)	Special	11.21 Mercury ☿ enters Cancer ♋ 18.43 Mars ♂ enters Leo ♌
Moon sign	♍		
Colour	Blue		
Herb or incense	Lavender		

Sunday 4th			
Moon quarter	2nd (waxing)	Herb or incense	Jasmine
Moon sign	♍	Crystal	Tiger's Eye
Colour	Indigo	Sun sign	♊

Father's Day Spell

Purpose of ritual: to give thanks for your father's love.
What you need: Father's Day card, gold pen.

In today's world, a father is no longer automatically the family provider and protector. As men accept their change of role in society, they can start to feel redundant and lacking a defined area of expertise.

Although we may not always see eye to eye with our dads, Father's Day gives us the opportunity to spoil them. Tell your dad how much you love and need him and what a great job he's doing. Treat your dad to a day out he will enjoy, and buy him a special card with which to work this simple spell.

- Take the card to your altar and light the candles. Breathe deeply until you feel centred and then, using a gold pen, write a personal message to your dad in the card. Now say:

Bless my dad who tries so hard. Bestow my love through this card. Let him see and let him know. That through his love I thrive and grow. So mote it be.

- Seal the card and give it to your dad on Father's Day.

To Call Back an Old Flame

Purpose of ritual: to make contact with an old flame
What you need: a photo of your ex, or an item that belonged to them, or their full name written on red or pink paper; your pentacle; your wand; a red envelope

- Make your altar room very romantic, for example by lighting red and pink candles and burning a floral oil. Add vases of flowers, play soft romantic music and scatter flower petals on the floor.
- Place the object that represents your old flame on your pentacle and sit for a while in silent meditation.
- Now spend time recalling the time you spent together. Drink your old flame's favourite wine, read a love poem that reminds you of them, watch a film or listen to music that you enjoyed together.
- Next, sit and think deeply of all that you loved about them, all that attracted you. Remember their appearance and the words they said to you. Remember their voice, the look in their eyes and their sweet names for you. Re-read any diaries from that time. Move your wand in a clockwise direction over the object that represents your ex and chant these words:

Before the moon is full six times more,
You will be knocking at my door.

- Continue chanting for as long as you can, then place the photograph in the red envelope. Seal the envelope and keep it close to you. If you are meant to be with this person, your power will bring them to you. You may repeat the spell once more, six months from now, as old flames can be very stubborn! But if you have heard nothing within a year, this meeting is not for your highest good. Remember the happy times and move on: an even greater love is waiting for you.

June

Dawn 03.51
Dusk 20.08

Monday 5th

Moon quarter	2nd (waxing)	Crystal	Sodalite
Moon sign	♍ 09.08 ♎	Sun sign	♊
Colour	Black	Special	World Environment Day
Herb or incense	Borage		

Tuesday 6th

Moon quarter	2nd (waxing)	Herb or incense	Fennel
Moon sign	♎	Crystal	Aventurine
Colour	Green	Sun sign	♊

Wednesday 7th

Moon quarter	2nd (waxing)	Herb or incense	Mugwort
Moon sign	♎ 20.41 ♏	Crystal	Carnelian
Colour	Silver	Sun sign	♊

Thursday 8th

Moon quarter	2nd (waxing)	Herb or incense	Angelica
Moon sign	♏	Crystal	Hematite
Colour	Pink	Sun sign	♊

Friday 9th

Moon quarter	2nd (waxing)	Herb or incense	Catnip
Moon sign	♏	Crystal	Jasper
Colour	Peach	Sun sign	♊

Saturday 10th

Moon quarter	2nd (waxing)	Herb or incense	Mace
Moon sign	♏ 05.05 ♐	Crystal	Amethyst
Colour	Yellow	Sun sign	♊

Sunday 11th

Moon phase	○	Herb or incense	Thyme
Time	18.03	Crystal	Moonstone
Moon quarter	3rd (waning)	Sun sign	♊
Moon sign	♐	Special	Dryad Moon
Colour	Purple		

DRYAD MOON

The full moon of June is known as the dryad moon. The dryads are the elemental life force of trees, and each tree has its own guardian dryad. The ancient Celts had a special relationship with these elementals and would invoke their presence in battle. If you have trees in your garden, make an effort to get to know the dryads. Sit beneath the tree if you can, and just silently acknowledge the presence of the tree elementals. Spend time with the trees regularly, and eventually the dryads will make themselves known to you. Always remember to leave an offering of some sort beneath the tree. This completes the exchange of energy. Your offering could be a shiny penny or a crystal, but usually a more natural gift is given. A libation of beer, milk or cream could be poured into the earth at the roots of the tree, or a saucer of honey could be left. Perhaps the most appropriate offering would be one that feeds the wildlife that lives in a tree. A mixture of nuts, sunflower seeds, breadcrumbs, bird seeds, currants and raisins, perhaps with little chunks of cheese and strips of bacon rind, would be appreciated by your local wildlife!

Try to commune with the dryads every day. Once you have established a relationship, you could tie wish ribbons to a tree's branches, asking that its elemental helps you to manifest your dreams.

Wish Bubbles

Blowing wish bubbles is definitely one of my favourite quickie spells. It's very simple and is a lovely way to use the breath of life in magic or to introduce magic to children or ritual-shy adults!

If you are going to use bubble magic quite often, invest in some 'tools'. Step into any toy shop and you will find some highly advanced bubble-making kits, together with bubble wands of various shapes and sizes. Experiment and see which brings about the best magical results.

If you feel a bit more grown-up about all this, you might like to invest in a bath spa and work magic with the water bubbles that it creates. Alternatively, to fill your home with bubble magic buy a small bubble-making machine. Empower the bubble mixture with your magical goal before adding it to the machine and then simply switch on and let the magic begin! This is a great way to magically enhance a party or to empower a group ritual held indoors.

Purpose of ritual: to make a wish come true
What you need: a small pot of magic bubbles

- Cleanse the bottle of bubbles by passing it through the smoke of your favourite incense. Ask that the spirits of air and water bless your magic and bring your spells to fruition.
- Take the bubbles with you to a quiet outdoor spot. Hold the bottle between your palms and concentrate on your magical goal.
- When you can see the desired outcome clearly in your mind, begin to blow bubbles, gently filling each bubble with your magical intention and the sacred breath of life. Keep your mind focused on your magical goal and your thoughts positive.
- Watch as the bubbles ride the wind, going out into the world. As each bubble pops, it releases the spell and the magic is in process.
- Before returning home, leave an offering to enhance the spell.

SUN MOVES INTO CANCER

On June 21st the sun moves into the sign of Cancer, which is ruled by the moon. The ruling stone for this sign is the moonstone – a beautiful feminine stone – while the birth stone is the pearl. Cancerians are generally quite cautious and need to feel protected and secure. They tend to show the world their hard, outer shell and keep their vulnerable side well hidden.

The moon phases have a particularly deep effect on Cancerians, and at sensitive points in the lunar cycle misunderstandings can occur. To people born under other signs, Cancerians can appear just plain moody. At their best, however, those born under this sign are tender-hearted friends and sympathetic listeners. They are also extremely protective of their loved ones – they don't have claws for nothing!

June

Dawn 03.51
Dusk 20.08

Monday 12th			
Moon quarter	3rd (waning)	Herb or incense	Dill
Moon sign	♐ 10.19 ♑	Crystal	Snowy Quartz
Colour	Orange	Sun sign	♊

Tuesday 13th			
Moon quarter	3rd (waning)	Herb or incense	Pine
Moon sign	♑	Crystal	Citrine
Colour	Jade	Sun sign	♊

Wednesday 14th			
Moon quarter	3rd (waning)	Herb or incense	Sage
Moon sign	♑ 13.32 ♒	Crystal	Bloodstone
Colour	Indigo	Sun sign	♊

Thursday 15th			
Moon quarter	3rd (waning)	Herb or incense	Valerian
Moon sign	♒	Crystal	Kunzite
Colour	Grey	Sun sign	♊

Friday 16th			
Moon quarter	3rd (waning)	Herb or incense	Cinnamon
Moon sign	♒ 16.05 ♓	Crystal	Sodalite
Colour	White	Sun sign	♊

Saturday 17th			
Moon quarter	3rd (waning)	Herb or incense	Sage
Moon sign	♓	Crystal	Hematite
Colour	Red	Sun sign	♊

Sunday 18th			
Moon phase	◑	Colour	Brown
Time	14.08	Herb or incense	Ginger
Moon quarter	4th (waning)	Crystal	Obsidian
Moon sign	♓ 18.54 ♈	Sun sign	♊

LITHA

At last the longest day has arrived! We have reached the height of summer, when the powers of the Sun God are at their strongest.

The summer solstice is known among witches as Litha. At this sabbat, which honours the power of the sun, decorate your altar with objects that bear the sun's image – candle holders, lanterns and oil burners. Place a deep yellow or gold cloth over your altar surface and add lots of gold candles. Vases of buttercups and sunflowers look fabulous on a Litha altar, as do citrine and amber crystals. Add yellow and gold ribbons, and maybe a daisy chain around the edge.

At Litha, witches also honour the glorious abundance of Mother Earth, and our altars reflect this in many ways. They may include a bowl of fruit or vegetables, a decanter of mead or a picture of an Earth goddess such as Gaia or Demeter. To honour the witches' God you might like to add a picture or statue that represents him. You can also include a small fairy statue to acknowledge the fey – Litha is the strongest time for workings of faery magic.

Celebrations should be held outdoors in the sun and can include faery magic, barbecues and perhaps a visit to a sacred site such as a stone circle. Burn this month's herbs and oils, decorate trees and local wells with flower garlands and ribbons while making a magical wish, or re-enact the battle between the Holly King and the Oak King. Finish your celebration with song and dance, and a feast of wonderful summer foods and orange juice – liquid sunshine!

June

Dawn 03.50
Dusk 20.12

Monday 19th

Moon quarter	4th (waning)	Herb or incense	Fennel
Moon sign	♈	Crystal	Red Jasper
Colour	White	Sun sign	♊

Tuesday 20th

Moon quarter	4th (waning)	Herb or incense	Jasmine
Moon sign	♈ 22.23 ♉	Crystal	Carnelian
Colour	Blue	Sun sign	♊

Wednesday 21st

Moon quarter	4th (waning)	Crystal	Jasper
Moon sign	♉	Sun sign	♊ 12.46 ♋
Colour	Gold	Special	Litha (summer
Herb or incense	Rosemary		solstice 12.26)

Thursday 22nd

Moon quarter	4th (waning)	Crystal	Amber
Moon sign	♉	Sun sign	♋
Colour	Green	Special	Final witchcraft law
Herb or incense	Sage		in England repealed 1951

Friday 23rd

Moon quarter	4th (waning)	Herb or incense	Fennel
Moon sign	♉ 02.49 ♊	Crystal	Tiger's Eye
Colour	Brown	Sun sign	♋

Saturday 24th

Moon quarter	4th (waning)	Crystal	Snowflake-Obsidian
Moon sign	♊	Sun sign	♋
Colour	Silver	Special	Aztec Feast of the Sun
Herb or incense	Bayberry		00.31 Venus ♀ enters Gemini ♊

Sunday 25th

Moon phase	●	Colour	Orange
Time	16.05	Herb or incense	Lavender
Moon quarter	1st (waxing	Crystal	Carnelian
Moon sign	♊ 08.48 ♋	Sun sign	♋

Soul Song

Music has a profound effect on our emotions and our state of mind. It has the power to make us happy, invigorated, restful, sleepy, calm, meditative or passionate. The beat of a drum connects us with the slow, steady heart beat of Mother Earth. The tapping of fingers and toes links us with the eternal dance of life. We raise our voice in song and our spirit lifts. Music crosses all boundaries and can transport us into the depth of a culture very different from our own. I have only to hear the music and chants of the Native Americans to be swept away to the Great Plains, seeing the buffalo in the distance and feeling the sun warm on my skin as the wind lifts braided hair dressed with beads and feathers. Music can evoke strong memories too. My mother is an avid Elvis fan, and hearing his music immediately takes me back to my childhood home.

Take a few moments now to think about your own tastes in music. Who do you dance to? Who do you make love to? Who do you cry to? I firmly believe that every one of us has a soul song. This is a song or piece of music that truly touches us, that reaches down into the very depths and core of our being. It helps us to celebrate the good times and comforts us through the bad times. It is a song that we never tire of listening to. Maybe you already know your own soul song; perhaps you will need to do some investigating to find it.

To give you a clue how to recognise it, my own soul song is one that I have loved since the tender age of 11 and is a song by A-HA called 'Hunting High and Low'. I can listen to it over and over and over again – and I do! It is the sweetest lullaby, the warmest comfort, the joy of life or the darkness of sleep after a really long day. This is the effect of a soul song and you can use it to powerful effect during magic and ritual.

To discover your own soul song, spend an evening alone in your altar room and work your way through your CDs (it may take more than one evening if you have a large collection!). Light the candles on your altar and burn incense if you like, but concentrate on the music. Once you have found your soul song, listen to it as often as you can, and make sure you hear it at least once in the hour before all your magical rituals. This will enhance any magic you do, uplifting your spirit and putting you in the positive frame of mind that is essential for magic and spell-casting.

June

Dawn 03.51
Dusk 20.13

Monday 26th			
Moon quarter	1st (waxing)	Herb or incense	Dill
Moon sign	♋	Crystal	Rose Quartz
Colour	Blue	Sun sign	♋

Tuesday 27th			
Moon quarter	1st (waxing)	Herb or incense	Pine
Moon sign	♋ 17.09 ♌	Crystal	Bloodstone
Colour	Brown	Sun sign	♋

Wednesday 28th			
Moon quarter	1st (waxing)	Crystal	Moonstone
Moon sign	♌	Sun sign	♋
Colour	Red	Special	19.57 Mercury ☿ enters Leo ♌
Herb or incense	Ginger		

Thursday 29th			
Moon quarter	1st (waxing)	Herb or incense	Mace
Moon sign	♌	Crystal	Citrine
Colour	Pink	Sun sign	♋

Friday 30th			
Moon quarter	1st (waxing)	Herb or incense	Angelica
Moon sign	♌ 04.15 ♍	Crystal	Amber
Colour	Jade	Sun sign	♋

The Enchanted Pool

Gaze in the enchanted pool and see
Reflections of your destiny –
Whether a prince or a pauper you'll make,
Or a handsome knight your hand will take.
Joys and sorrows, all are here;
Simply bend over the water and peer.
Your own reflection will gradually fade,
Instead you will see how your fortune is made.
Here is your future laid out like a map,
Allowing you time to avoid mishap.
But only if your heart is pure and true
Will you see how to make your dreams come true.

July

The sun is still shining bright and clear, and we are enjoying all that summer has to offer. Now that the summer solstice has passed, however, we are aware that these long days will not last much longer, and we must make the most of them. In the Wiccan calendar July is a month of rest after the hectic festivities of Litha. It is one of the few months of the year that does not contain a sabbat or festival of some kind, and many witches see it as a month for quiet reflection on all that the year has brought so far.

July is the month of the hazel tree. Revered as a tree of intuition by the ancient Celts, who called it coll, the hazel was also much respected by the Druids. This tree has long been associated with magic, particularly aspects of divination, and in some cultures it was believed that to eat hazel nuts would bring about prophetic visions. It is for this reason that many divination tools, such as runes for example, are crafted from hazel wood. It is also a wood much favoured for magical wands.

The hazel is also seen as a tree of wisdom and inspiration. It bears the country name 'poet's tree', and it is believed that communing with its dryad can enhance creativity and self-expression – so if you are of an artistic turn, you might like to spend some time with the hazel spirit. To include this magical tree in your spell-castings, look for a hazel wand, or craft a pentacle or set of runes from hazel wood.

The flower of July is the beautiful cornflower, which, according to the Victorian language of flowers, symbolises delicacy. The wisdom of the cornflower tells us to tread carefully and to take our time rather than rushing through things. Add a vase of cornflowers to your altar or meditation room, and perhaps mix them with this month's herb, lavender. An arrangement of lavender and cornflowers in the bedroom will look wonderful, and the delightful fragrance will aid restful sleep.

Fennel is another herb associated with the month of July and can be used in all protection rituals, as traditionally it is believed to have the power to ward off evil.

July

Dawn 03.51
Dusk 20.13

Saturday 1st			
Moon quarter	1st (waxing)	Crystal	Clear Quartz
Moon sign	♍	Sun sign	♋
Colour	White	Special	Death of Nostradamus 1566
Herb or incense	Dill		

Sunday 2nd			
Moon quarter	1st (waxing)	Herb or incense	Mace
Moon sign	♍ 17.06 ♎	Crystal	Kunzite
Colour	Red	Sun sign	♋

Magical Mantra

Mantras and chants have long been used as a way of remaining focused in meditation. This technique can also be used to attract something into your life in a magical way.

If you meditate regularly, simply make your usual preparations. If meditation is new to you, here's how to go about it. It's important that you aren't disturbed, so put the cat out, turn off your mobile phone, turn on the answering machine, and lock your door. Meditation usually takes place in a quiet room. This could be your altar room or a different room altogether. If you have the luxury of space, you might like to create your own meditation room. Most of us, however, have to use a quiet corner of the house somewhere. I perform my meditations in the bedroom, which is also my main altar room.

In preparation, light your favourite incense and maybe put on a CD of meditational music. Pile cushions on the floor and settle down in a comfortable position. Steady your breathing and clear your head of thoughts. Now gently bring to mind the vision of what you are working towards. This could be love, wealth, health, freedom and so forth. Narrow your goal down to a single word and slowly and gently repeat that word as a mantra, taking a full breath in between repetitions. If your word is quite long, break it up into syllables, for example, ah-bun-dance (abundance). Continue this mantra, strongly visualising yourself enjoying your magical goal.

Repeat the meditation daily until your goal manifests. Remember to keep your thoughts entirely positive and to keep breathing.

Mead Libation

As with all the rituals and spells in this book, feel free to change or re-word anything in this libation that you feel uncomfortable with. Take the bones of the concept and make the ritual your own.

Purpose of ritual:	to ask the Goddess for help with your troubles
What you need:	a stick of Night Queen incense, your chalice, a little mead, a CD of quiet music – for example goddess chants (optional)

- Go to your altar or Triple Goddess shrine and light the candles there. Light a stick of Night Queen incense and settle down, perhaps on a cushion or chair.
- Meditate silently for a few minutes to clear your mind, and then begin to commune with the witches' Goddess. Tell her your troubles and ask for assistance with any life challenges you are currently facing. Give thanks for all that you are grateful for.
- Now take up your magical chalice and pour a little of the mead into it. Lift it high and say:

  I ask the Goddess, Mother of All, great provider and Queen of Abundance, to fill my cup.

- Take the chalice outside to a sacred spot in your garden, perhaps beneath a tree or by a well, and pour the mead into the earth – this is the libation. Say these words or similar:

  I give to the great Mother that the Mother may give to me.
  So be it! Blessed be!

- Return to your altar and continue in meditation, listening to the CD if you have chosen to use one.
- Once you feel your ritual is complete, extinguish the candles and go about your day.

July

Dawn 03.55
Dusk 20.12

Monday 3rd

Moon phase	◐	Colour	Silver
Time	16.37	Herb or incense	Frankincense
Moon quarter	2nd (waxing)	Crystal	Amethyst
Moon sign	♎	Sun sign	♋

Tuesday 4th

Moon quarter	2nd (waxing)	Herb or incense	Borage
Moon sign	♎	Crystal	Sodalite
Colour	Brown	Sun sign	♋

Wednesday 5th

Moon quarter	2nd (waxing)	Herb or incense	Bay
Moon sign	♎ 05.13 ♏	Crystal	Aventurine
Colour	Pink	Sun sign	♋

Thursday 6th

Moon quarter	2nd (waxing)	Herb or incense	Lavender
Moon sign	♏	Crystal	Topaz
Colour	Yellow	Sun sign	♋

Friday 7th

Moon quarter	2nd (waxing)	Herb or incense	Jasmine
Moon sign	♏ 14.14 ♐	Crystal	Amber
Colour	Green	Sun sign	♋

Saturday 8th

Moon quarter	2nd (waxing)	Herb or incense	Sage
Moon sign	♐	Crystal	Jasper
Colour	Black	Sun sign	♋

Sunday 9th

Moon quarter	2nd (waxing)	Herb or incense	Mugwort
Moon sign	♐ 19.25 ♑	Crystal	Red Jasper
Colour	Orange	Sun sign	♋

Weather Witching

Since ancient times witches have been accused of altering the weather patterns to suit their own needs. While it's true that witches do work with the weather, performing the odd rain spell or sunny day ritual, we do not control it. What we do do is connect with the elementals and ask for their assistance. A weather spell will only be effective if the elementals agree that the weather we are spelling for is actually needed.

While I was writing this book, the weather was unusually hot for a fairly long time. While most people were enjoying the mini heat wave, the earth was drying, the wildlife was suffering and I was going quietly mad! I am not a summer person at all. I much prefer the biting winds and hoar frosts of winter. So I decided to do a little weather witching in the form of a rain spell – well, three to be exact! You might say I got a little carried away! All that day I waited, and still the weather did not break. There were one or two rumbles of thunder, but not a drop of moisture in the air. Finally, during the night, the weather broke with a fabulously heavy downpour of rain. In fact we had exactly three full days of torrential rain. One for each spell? I don't know, but it will teach me not to be so over-enthusiastic! In truth though, the earth must have needed the rain or the elementals wouldn't have brought it. That's the way weather magic works.

As the British weather can change in an instant, that is usually how long witches have to think up a quickie spell and work weather magic. Here are some quick weather spells for you to experiment with. Always remember to visualise the particular elemental you are contacting, and to work with harm to none and a deep respect for nature.

- To call a particular wind, face that direction (for example, North) and whistle or play a wind instrument such as the flute or pan pipes. This is known as 'whistling in the wind'.

- To bring rain, empower a bowl of water with your intent, focus on the undines and water sprites, and then throw the water high into the air – you may get a little wet with this one!

- To call out the sun, light a tea-light and place it in a lantern outdoors, while focusing hard on the salamanders, spirits of fire. Alternatively, take a bright torch and shine it into the sky, asking the sun to come out.

- To avert storm damage, ask the spirits of the storm to pass over your property without destruction and with harm to none.

Other forms of weather magic

- Collect gentle spring rains in a bowl and use them in magical potions or baths. Do the same with winter snows.
- Take an icicle and empower it with your goal. Place it in the sink or bath. As it begins to melt, the magic begins.

MEAD MOON

The full moon of July is called the mead moon. Mead is a wonderful warming beverage. It is reputed to have been the very first alcoholic drink and was the toast of many ancient peoples, including the Egyptians, Saxons, Romans, Greeks, Celts and Vikings.

Mead is a frequent ingredient in magic and rituals. It is made from honey and so is used to connect with the Goddess. In the past, it was drunk for its intoxicating effect, which enabled magical workers to commune with the gods and aided visions, pathworkings and meditations. Mead is also a staple in old fertility spells. In fact the word 'honeymoon' comes from the practice of newly wed couples drinking mead each day for one lunar month after their marriage. This was believed to increase chances of early conception. The custom illustrates a further link between mead, the moon and therefore the witches' goddess. If you would like to try mead, it can be bought from most large off-licences (over 18s only!). It's a nice idea to keep a small amount of mead on your altar for use in ritual. This should be stored in a pretty decanter, perhaps with a measuring cup nearby, just to be on the safe side! Mead is also excellent for libations.

July

Dawn 04.01 Dusk 20.09

Monday 10th

Moon quarter	2nd (waxing)	Crystal	Tiger's Eye
Moon sign	♑	Sun sign	♋
Colour	Brown	Special	Lady Godiva's ride
Herb or incense	Fennel		20.18 Mercury ☿ enters Cancer ♋

Tuesday 11th

Moon phase	○	Herb or incense	Catnip
Time	03.02	Crystal	Carnelian
Moon quarter	3rd (waning)	Sun sign	♋
Moon sign	♑ 21.46 ♒	Special	Mead Moon
Colour	Blue		

Wednesday 12th

Moon quarter	3rd (waning)	Herb or incense	Mint
Moon sign	♒	Crystal	Rose Quartz
Colour	Purple	Sun sign	♋

Thursday 13th

Moon quarter	3rd (waning)	Herb or incense	Angelica
Moon sign	♒ 22.59 ♓	Crystal	Snowy Quartz
Colour	Jade	Sun sign	♋

Friday 14th

Moon quarter	3rd (waning)	Sun sign	♋
Moon sign	♓	Special	First recorded appearance of crop circles, Silbury Hill, England 1988
Colour	Blue		
Herb or incense	Parsley		
Crystal	Snowflake-Obsidian		

Saturday 15th

Moon quarter	3rd (waning)	Herb or incense	Valerian
Moon sign	♓	Crystal	Smokey Quartz
Colour	Pink	Sun sign	♋

Sunday 16th

Moon quarter	3rd (waning)	Herb or incense	Lavender
Moon sign	♓ 00.39 ♈	Crystal	Hematite
Colour	Indigo	Sun sign	♋

July

Dawn 04.08
Dusk
20.03

Monday 17th			
Moon phase	◑	Colour	Peach
Time	19.13	Herb or incense	Fennel
Moon quarter	4th (waning)	Crystal	Obsidian
Moon sign	♈	Sun sign	♋

Tuesday 18th			
Moon quarter	4th (waning)	Herb or incense	Angelica
Moon sign	♈ 03.44 ♉	Crystal	Moonstone
Colour	Gold	Sun sign	♋

Wednesday 19th			
Moon quarter	4th (waning)	Crystal	Citrine
Moon sign	♉	Sun sign	♋
Colour	Brown	Special	02.41 Venus ♀
Herb or incense	Sage		enters Cancer ♋

Thursday 20th			
Moon quarter	4th (waning)	Herb or incense	Thyme
Moon sign	♉ 08.38 ♊	Crystal	Bloodstone
Colour	Grey	Sun sign	♋

Friday 21st			
Moon quarter	4th (waning)	Herb or incense	Fennel
Moon sign	♊	Crystal	Kunzite
Colour	Silver	Sun sign	♋

Saturday 22nd			
Moon quarter	4th (waning)	Crystal	Jasper
Moon sign	♊ 15.28 ♋	Sun sign	♋ 23.18 ♌
Colour	Blue	Special	18.53 Mars ♂
Herb or incense	Mugwort		enters Virgo ♍

Sunday 23rd			
Moon quarter	4th (waning)	Herb or incense	Ginger
Moon sign	♋	Crystal	Topaz
Colour	Peach	Sun sign	♌

SUN MOVES INTO LEO

On July 22nd the sun enters Leo, a sign that is ruled by the sun. The birth stone for Leo is the ruby, and the power stone is tiger's eye. Leos are often filled with a sense of righteous nobility and are almost entirely focused on the bigger picture. As they are ruled by the sun, they are warm-hearted with a naturally sunny disposition and can be generous to a fault!

Due to the influence of the sun's energy, however, Leos can be a little superior and like to be at the centre of their own universe, occasionally expecting everyone else to revolve around them like planets! At their most positive though, Leos are strong, loyal, creative, positive and generous people who have a lot to give and will always support a friend in need.

River Stone Ritual

For this lovely little healing ritual, you will need to go to a river or stream. If you'd like to make a day of it, you could take an excursion out to the countryside and use it as sacred time. Alternatively, you can work this spell by the sea. Go with like-minded friends or by yourself – it's up to you. As the purpose of the ritual is to remove something from your life, choose a time when the moon is waning to perform it.

Purpose of ritual: to remove something unwanted from your life.

- Once you have discovered your ritual site, sit by the water and paddle your feet. Commune with the undines and know that the waters of the earth are considered to be the life-force that connects all things. As you do this, scan the river bed for a stone or pebble that looks appealing, or wait for the waves to cast one to you.
- When you have located your stone, pick it up and hold it between your palms, settling yourself once more by the water.
- Concentrate fully on the negative aspect of your life that you wish to be free from. Focus your attention on sending the negativity into the pebble in your hand.
- Once you feel you have released all the negativity, cast the pebble back into the water and ask the spirits of water to heal you. Your ritual is now concluded.

Wishing Well Magic

Wishing wells have always had a place in magic and have long been held sacred to the Goddess, as they reach down into the depths of Mother Earth. The act of tossing a coin into a body of water and asking for our heart's desire is an ancient way of invoking the power of the water elementals. I can clearly remember, as a very small child, standing at the mouth of a wishing well, and making the heart-felt plea, 'I wish for a dog!' I was delighted when my coin struck the brass bell contained within the well (another symbol of the Pagan Goddess), as I knew it was a sure sign that my wish had been heard and would come true. Sure enough, a few months later my parents bought a beautiful Chihuahua puppy. We called him Pepe and I loved him to bits! He was my companion throughout childhood and definitely a dream come true.

Magically speaking, a wishing well connects us with the undines who are the elementals of water. As we ask these magical forces to assist us in manifesting our dreams, we give them an offering, usually a coin, as a payment for their help. Of course, you may not have an ancient sacred well to hand, but there are several ways you can create your own wishing well for use in magic.

The most obvious way is to buy a small decorative well and set it in a corner of your garden or on a balcony. Dedicate the well to the undines and consecrate it with a splash of water mixed with a little sea salt. It is now a magical tool. You can decorate it with flowers and ribbons, place a statue of a goddess at its base and perhaps hang windchimes, mirrors and crystals from its roof. Then either fill the well with pure spring water or wait for it to be filled with rain. If you have the space and like your home to look unusual, you can even set up a small well like this indoors.

Alternatively, you could invest in a beautiful blue or green vessel and place this on your altar. Fill it with spring water, perhaps adding a little turquoise food colouring, and place pebbles, sea-shells and perhaps add a beautiful faceted crystal or two.

Repeat this spell each time you use your well:

Water spirit, water sprite,
I make this wish with all my might.
Water spirit, water sprite,
Grant the wish I make this night.

Make your wish by the light of the moon and throw in a coin. Every so often, donate the coins to your favourite charity.

Exercise to Increase Inner Strength

I believe that we all have a deep source of inner strength and that I can use it to handle anything if we have the right attitude.

Building up inner strength is an ongoing process. The trick is to constantly surround yourself with things that represent strength to you on a personal level. There are no right or wrong things; your choice will be unique. For example, the film *Braveheart* always makes me feel that I can tackle anything, and win! You may see strength in something from nature, lions perhaps, or you may feel inspired by a particular activity, such as dancing or running.

My home is filled with things that inspire me to be strong. In history, I'm inspired by the Scottish clansmen who fought for liberty – what can I say? I'm a Bruce! – and I have a collection of figures depicting such heroes as Wallace, Bruce and Rob Roy. In mythology, dragons and armoured knights make me think of strength and courage. Dragon power oozes from my dragon altar and dragon statues, and I have a collection of fine art prints depicting knights in armour, arranged around a wooden shield and a small sword. In nature I love towering trees, and I have a collection of oak leaf men and Green Man wall plaques, as well as a lovely pewter candle stand that is fashioned to look like a bare-branched tree in winter. All these things help me to realise that strength comes in many forms and many guises. I look around my home and strength is reflected back at me from every corner.

Take some time now to think of everything that speaks to you of strength. Remember that this is entirely a personal exercise. If you feel drawn to a particular animal or natural landscape, then begin to collect images of it. Place them near you when you sleep, put them on your desk at work and meditate on them when you are experiencing challenges or when your positive attitude has been weakened. Think up an affirmation that reminds you of your inner strength and that will instil you with courage as you work your way through difficult days.

Sometimes it can be hard to maintain a positive attitude. If you ever find yourself in a traumatic situation with no idea what to do, try to make a conscious shift in attitude, use the affirmation you've created and evoke your personal strength. Trust in that strength, and in yourself, and you will find a way through.

July

Dawn 04.17
Dusk 19.56

Monday 24th

Moon quarter	4th (waning)	Herb or incense	Catnip
Moon sign	♋	Crystal	Sodalite
Colour	White	Sun sign	♌

Tuesday 25th

Moon phase	●	Colour	Pink
Time	04.31	Herb or incense	Mace
Moon quarter	1st (waxing)	Crystal	Obsidian
Moon sign	♋ 00.24 ♌	Sun sign	♌

Wednesday 26th

Moon quarter	1st (waxing)	Herb or incense	Dill
Moon sign	♌	Crystal	Hematite
Colour	Green	Sun sign	♌

Thursday 27th

Moon quarter	1st (waxing)	Herb or incense	Mint
Moon sign	♌ 11.36 ♍	Crystal	Red Jasper
Colour	Purple	Sun sign	♌

Friday 28th

Moon quarter	1st (waxing)	Herb or incense	Fennel
Moon sign	♍	Crystal	Carnelian
Colour	Gold	Sun sign	♌

Saturday 29th

Moon quarter	1st (waxing)	Herb or incense	Valerian
Moon sign	♍	Crystal	Aventurine
Colour	Red	Sun sign	♌

Sunday 30th

Moon quarter	1st (waxing)	Herb or incense	Jasmine
Moon sign	♍ 00.27 ♎	Crystal	Topaz
Colour	Green	Sun sign	♌

Monday 31st			
Moon quarter	1st (waxing)	Herb or incense	Cinnamon
Moon sign	♎	Crystal	Amethyst
Colour	Orange	Sun sign	♌

A WICCAN TIME CAPSULE

A great way to record the events of a year is to create a time capsule. This is basically a collection of items and mementos that symbolise events in your life and the given year. You can make a Wiccan time capsule by gathering objects that have a magical significance. First find or buy a special box, or decorate an old shoe box. Then write your full name, magical name, date of birth and your current age and the year on a decorative label and attach this to the box.

As you go through the year fill the box with magical items such as dated newspaper reports of crop circles, meteor showers, solar and lunar eclipses, or other magical or significant events. You could also include photos of yourself, your Craft friends or coven, and your familiar, as well as tickets to Wiccan festivals, picture postcards of sacred sites you have visited, copies of spells you have cast that worked particularly well or had a significant effect on your life, sea shells from your holidays, pictures or postcards that represent your favourite witchy film or television series of the year, a written record of a particular dream you have had, details of gods, goddesses, elementals or spirit guides you have discovered an affinity with. Anything that has a magical significance in your life can go into the box.

By the end of the year you will have a box of items that sum up your magical life over the last 12 months. You may even decide to begin a new time capsule every year as a means of charting your progress on your personal magical path.

River Siren

Beneath the tranquil, turquoise waters,
Shyly hidden among the reeds,
There lives one of Neptune's daughters,
Whose lonely heart slowly bleeds.

She dreams of life, she dreams of love
From the depths of her watery cell;
There she rests in a sandy cove
And sleeps in an oyster shell.

Her skin is of the palest pearl
That softly gleams and shimmers;
The tresses of her hair unfurl,
And in her eye a tear glimmers.

An enchanting song is heard so often,
Sung by the damsel of the deep.
She is the mysterious River Siren,
Left beneath the waves to weep.

To weep for the love she'll never know,
To sorrow for the life she craves,
To wait for the man who'll sink so low
To love her beneath the waves.

August

The late summer sun sends an amber glow across the fields of golden wheat. Hibernating creatures spend the last weeks of summer storing food and generally preparing for the long winter ahead. The occasional chill wind or shower of rain gives us the first hint of autumn. August is a month of preparation.

The harvests are brought in, final repairs to homes and property are taken care of to ensure security through the darker days ahead, store cupboards are checked and stocked up. At the same time, we make the most of the warmth that is left, perhaps indulging in a holiday or weekend break. To witches, August is the month of thanksgiving, when we honour the sacrifice of the Corn God in the sabbat of Lughnasadh.

In the Celtic Ogham, August is the month of the vine (muin), whose fruit has been used for centuries to make wine. The vine itself is symbolic of joy and euphoria, and in the past wine was often drunk as a part of ritual to enhance divinations and vision quests. It is for this reason that the vine was considered to release the psychic powers of the prophet. The Celts also associated the vine with the darkness of the Underworld, and in this sense the plant is connected to darker goddesses such as Mabd, the Morrigan, Hecate and Persephone.

The flower of August is the dahlia, which symbolises dignity, and the herbs are fennel and patchouli, both known for their protective properties and ability to enhance psychism.

August

Dawn 04.26
Dusk 19.47

Tuesday 1st

Moon quarter	1st (waxing	Sun sign	♌
Moon sign	♎ 13.08 ♏	Special	Horse's Birthday (southern hemisphere) Lammas/Lughnasadh
Colour	Gold		
Herb or incense	Frankincense		
Crystal	Amber		

Wednesday 2nd

Moon phase	◐	Colour	Brown
Time	08.46	Herb or incense	Thyme
Moon quarter	2nd (waxing)	Crystal	Jasper
Moon sign	♏	Sun sign	♌

Thursday 3rd

Moon quarter	2nd (waxing)	Herb or incense	Pine
Moon sign	♏ 23.13 ♐	Crystal	Tiger's Eye
Colour	Orange	Sun sign	♌

Friday 4th

Moon quarter	2nd (waxing)	Herb or incense	Mugwort
Moon sign	♐	Crystal	Carnelian
Colour	Green	Sun sign	♌

Saturday 5th

Moon quarter	2nd (waxing)	Herb or incense	Jasmine
Moon sign	♐	Crystal	Rose Quartz
Colour	Purple	Sun sign	♌

Sunday 6th

Moon quarter	2nd (waxing)	Herb or incense	Rosemary
Moon sign	♐ 05.19 ♑	Crystal	Hematite
Colour	Blue	Sun sign	♌

LUGHNASADH

The sabbat of Lughnasadh (pronounced Loo-nas-ah) is the first harvest festival of the year. In times past the harvest would have been central to everyone's lives, and all members of the community would have turned out to help cut the fields and see their bounty brought in. In modern society most of us are more removed from the harvest, and it can often pass by without our even being aware of it. Sabbats such as Lughnasadh are a way for Pagans to keep in touch with the cycle of the seasons.

Lughnasadh is named after the Celtic sun god Lugh, and is largely centred on the sacrifice of the Corn King, John Barleycorn, the spirit of the harvest who is cut down each year to feed the people yet returns the following summer. Symbols of death and rebirth, then, are a part of this festival, and ancient ritual practices often involved some form of symbolic sacrifice.

Druids, for instance, would build a large wicker effigy of a man, which would then be burnt on a huge bonfire. Many country folk would give the last sheaf of wheat or corn in sacrifice and as an offering of thanks. In very ancient times the king himself is said to have gone willingly to his death to provide for his people, at a time when it was believed that the king and the land were one.

Of course, modern sabbat celebrations contain nothing so dramatic. We work symbolic magic of protection and set our altars up to reflect the colours of the season and the Corn God. A deep burnt yellow or bronze altar cloth is appropriate, and some form of harvest should be placed upon it. Choose perhaps a loaf or rice cakes, hedgerow fruits or seeds and nuts. Incense and candles and a representation of the God, perhaps Herne the Hunter, should also be included.

Lughnasadh Ritual

I created this little ritual for myself and friends. It is simple yet meaningful, and could provide the blueprint for you to write your own rituals for this and other sabbats.

We performed this ritual late on the night of Lughnasadh. We stood beneath a large fir tree, which sheltered us from the rain that was falling quite heavily. The night was still, and the only sound was the raindrops and the ritual words echoing beneath the branches. It was a special moment in nature – and in our witchcraft and our friendship too.

Use this ritual with our love, adapt it to suit your own needs, and enjoy the Lughnasadh festival.

Purpose of ritual: to give thanks for all we have and to honour the Goddess and the God

What you need: a libation of mead, beer, milk or cream; an offering of bread, cornflakes or other breakfast cereal (to represent the harvest); some sticks of your favourite incense; matches or a lighter; a lantern or torch (if you are working in the evening or at night); food for the feast – crusty cob sandwiches (with a stick man carved into the top to represent the Corn God), berries, fruits, chocolate rice cakes, corn cakes and gingerbread men (see page 159) would be appropriate

■ Stand beneath a tree and, all together, speak these words with strength and clarity:

Three witches stand together
On the sacred night of Lughnasadh
To honour the sacrifice of John Barleycorn,
To welcome the gifts of the harvest home.
In praise and thanks we give to thee,
Beneath the boughs of the magical tree.
As above, so below.
By our will, it shall be so!

■ Now each of you in turn repeats the following words:

I give thanks for ---- (name something in your life you are grateful for). May it continue. So be it!

■ Repeat the following words all together:

Send our words out to the skies.
Feel the Wiccan power rise.
By Earth, by Wind, by Fire, by Water,
Hear the words of the Goddess's daughter.

■ Witch one leaves an offering of food beneath tree and says:

We give to the Earth that the Earth may give to us.
In perfect love and perfect trust. Blessed be!

■ Witch two pours a libation of mead beneath tree and says:

We give to the Goddess that the Goddess may give to us. In perfect love and perfect trust. Blessed be!

- Witch three lights the incense, stakes it in the ground and says:

We give to the universe that the universe may give to us. In perfect love and perfect trust. Blessed be!

- All three say together:

As summer fades to autumn's gold,
We begin to see our dreams unfold.
For the free will of all and with harm to none,
We say farewell to the God of Sun.
Spirit to spirit, heart to heart,
Merry we meet and merry we part,
In honour of the Goddess and the God.
Blessed Be!

- Finish off your ritual with a feast. Once you have taken down your Circle and cleared up any litter, return indoors and settle down to chat with your friends, perhaps enjoying more mead and watching a film such as *The Wicker Man.*

Ritual of Thanks

Now that we have reached August it is time to give thanks for all that 2006 has brought us so far, good and bad.

Purpose of ritual: to give thanks for what the year has brought you
What you need: an essential oil, an oil burner, a pen, some slips of paper, a lighter or matches, your cauldron

- Go to your altar and light the illuminator candles. Set the essential oil burning and cast the Circle. Reflect on all the year has brought.
- Now pick out the three most significant things and write each one down on a separate slip of paper.
- Meditate on each one in turn. Why was this so important? How has it altered your life or attitude? How has it developed you as a person?
- Once you are comfortable with the effects this event has had on you, give thanks and burn the slip of paper in your cauldron.
- Go about your normal day, remembering that gratitude is one of the most powerful forms of magic you can work.

Harvest King Protection Powder

This powder uses the gift of the Corn God and the harvest, blended together with one or two staples of protection magic. It should be made just before Lughnasadh.

Purpose of ritual: to make a powder for protection

What you need: one weetabix, 1 tbsp cornflakes, 1 tbsp rice crispies, 1 tbsp black pepper, 1 tbsp garlic powder, 2 tsp dried basil, a mortar and pestle, your cauldron

- Using the mortar and pestle, grind up the weetabix, cornflakes and rice crispies.
- Pour this finely ground powder into your cauldron and add the black pepper and garlic powder (both for protection).
- Finally, mix in the dried basil, to add power and strength.
- Stir all the ingredients together, chanting the words:

Protected be!

- Place the cauldron on your altar and leave it there for the festival of Lughnasadh, when you can use the powder in protection rites. For example, a good way to protect your property is to sprinkle this powder around the perimeter of your garden, asking the spirits of the harvest to guard and protect your home with their energies. Sprinkle a little on outer windowsills, balconies, doorsteps and porches too, or roll a white candle in the powder as part of a protection spell.
- Transfer any remaining powder into an airtight container, label it and use it whenever you need.

WYRT MOON

The full moon of August is known as the wyrt moon – wyrt meaning 'green plant'. Now would be an excellent time to plant something in your garden and dedicate it to the Green Man.

August

Dawn 04.35
Dusk 19.35

Monday 7th			
Moon quarter	2nd (waxing)	Herb or incense	Catnip
Moon sign	♑	Crystal	Snowy Quartz
Colour	Yellow	Sun sign	♌

Tuesday 8th			
Moon quarter	2nd (waxing)	Herb or incense	Mace
Moon sign	♑ 07.47 ♒	Crystal	Smokey Quartz
Colour	Black	Sun sign	♌

Wednesday 9th			
Moon phase	○	Herb or incense	Ginger
Time	10.54	Crystal	Moonstone
Moon quarter	3rd (waning)	Sun sign	♌
Moon sign	♒	Special	Wyrt Moon
Colour	Pink		

Thursday 10th			
Moon quarter	3rd (waning)	Herb or incense	Angelica
Moon sign	♒ 08.10 ♓	Crystal	Citrine
Colour	Purple	Sun sign	♌

Friday 11th			
Moon quarter	3rd (waning)	Crystal	Bloodstone
Moon sign	♓	Sun sign	♌
Colour	Silver	Special	04.09 Mercury ☿ enters Leo ♌
Herb or incense	Cinnamon		

Saturday 12th			
Moon quarter	3rd (waning)	Crystal	Clear Quartz
Moon sign	♓ 08.22 ♈	Sun sign	♌
Colour	Jade	Special	20.21 Venus ♀ enters Leo ♌
Herb or incense	Nutmeg		

Sunday 13th			
Moon quarter	3rd (waning)	Herb or incense	Borage
Moon sign	♈	Crystal	Kunzite
Colour	Brown	Sun sign	♌

Shrine to the Green Man

Keep the positive protective energies of the Green Man around you and your home at all times by creating a shrine dedicated to his powers. This shrine could be a wild corner of your garden where you carve a fence post into the form of the head of the Green Man. Fix a pair of antlers to the top of the fence post and you have your very own Herne. Hang feathers, bells and crystals from the antlers and burn stick incense before the shrine.

If you feel that carving fence posts is beyond your skill, create a wall shrine on the side of your house by fixing up a weather-resistant Green Man wall plaque and hanging up a couple of wall lanterns. Alternatively, you might like to set up a simple shrine indoors. This could consist of a picture on the wall or one or two of the Green Man products on the market, such as a wall plaque or planter, or figure of Pan, Herne or Cernunos. If you prefer the Green Man in one of his many disguises look for pictures and statues that depict that character.

My own Green Man shrine is on top of my writer's bureau. On the wall above is a Green Man plaque – a face made up of oak leaves. On the bureau is a collection of smiling terracotta oak leaf men formed into candle-sticks, tea-light holders, trinket boxes and offering bowls. In one corner stands a little vase with a leaf design; this holds a collection of incense sticks, usually of a woodland fragrance such as pine. In the centre is a small grey tree stump carved with a wonderful tree-man face. On each side stands a pewter goblet, one resembling Gandalf and the other resembling Treebeard (both from *The Lord of the Rings*). Nearby is a beautiful green plant. Of course, a magical space like this doesn't come together overnight but evolves over a period of time, so be patient.

If you want to keep costs to a minimum, use a collection of pictures – for instance from a Robin Hood film, a basket of cones and acorns, a vase of twigs or a moss-covered stone. You can also use an indoor plant surrounded by crystals. Use your imagination. Light a candle and ask the energies of the Green Man to help you find things that are just right for you and your home.

Gingerbread Magic

Gingerbread men are a traditional food at this season of the year. You may have noticed that we included them in our Lughnasadh feast. This is because their human shape links them to the Corn God and thus to this sabbat.

In the Far East ginger has long been used to connect with the gods. In magic, too, it is known as a substance that can aid communion and is regularly used as an offering. The Lughnasadh gingerbread men, for example, can be used to commune with the sacrificed Corn God and with other harvest deities. Ginger can also be added to potions of love and healing, and is considered to give energy and relieve sickness.

This is another ritual that you might like to incorporate in your Lughnasadh celebrations.

Purpose of ritual: to commune with the Corn God
What you need: one gingerbread man per person, a plate, your pentacle, your athame

- Arrange the gingerbread men on a plate and place the plate on the altar, on top of your pentacle, to charge while you carry out your other sabbat work.
- At the end of your festival, as a final part of the feast, take up your gingerbread man and think of something you would like the harvest to bring you. Hold the gingerbread man firmly and focus your intention into him. Say the following charm:

Man of ginger, man of dough,
Take me where I want to go.
We honour now your sacrifice
And accept your gifts of grain and rice.
Let the harvest bring to me
All I want. So mote it be!

- Now, using your athame, cut the head of the gingerbread man clean off, in a symbolic re-enactment of the Corn God's sacrifice.
- Place the head as an offering on your Green Man shrine and leave it overnight, then put it outside in a wild place. Eat the rest of the gingerbread man to end the feast.

August

Dawn 04.46
Dusk 19.23

Monday 14th

Moon quarter	3rd (waning)	Herb or incense	Fennel
Moon sign	♈ 10.00 ♉	Crystal	Amethyst
Colour	White	Sun sign	♌

Tuesday 15th

Moon quarter	3rd (waning)	Herb or incense	Sage
Moon sign	♉	Crystal	Sodalite
Colour	Blue	Sun sign	♌

Wednesday 16th

Moon phase	◑	Colour	Peach
Time	01.51	Herb or incense	Dill
Moon quarter	4th (waning)	Crystal	Aventurine
Moon sign	♉ 14.07 ♊	Sun sign	♌

Thursday 17th

Moon quarter	4th (waning)	Herb or incense	Thyme
Moon sign	♊	Crystal	Topaz
Colour	Indigo	Sun sign	♌

Friday 18th

Moon quarter	4th (waning)	Herb or incense	Mace
Moon sign	♊ 21.03 ♋	Crystal	Jasper
Colour	Black	Sun sign	♌

Saturday 19th

Moon quarter	4th (waning)	Herb or incense	Mint
Moon sign	♋	Crystal	Obsidian
Colour	Pink	Sun sign	♌

Sunday 20th

Moon quarter	4th (waning)	Herb or incense	Pine
Moon sign	♋	Crystal	Carnelian
Colour	Silver	Sun sign	♌

To Empower Ginger Ale

Purpose of ritual: to empower ginger ale to use in autumn spells.
What you need: a bottle of ginger ale or ginger beer, your chalice

- Pour some ginger ale or ginger beer into your chalice. Hold your power hand (the one you write with) over the chalice and visualise a strong white light empowering the drink with your chosen goal.
- Once you feel that the drink is fully empowered, say these words:

Ginger beverage, liquid fire,
Grant to me my desire.

- Pour a tiny amount of the liquid into a potted plant or in your garden as a libation and then drink the rest, taking into yourself its magic and power.

Hope Chest

The Victorians had a charming tradition of creating hope chests. These were usually filled with household linens for a young woman awaiting marriage, or perhaps items laid by for the birth of a baby and put together with love by family and friends.

Why not create a magical hope chest to encourage self-empowerment and to take charge of your hopes and dreams? This can be a chest (a blanket box or ottoman) or it can be symbolic (a silver trinket box or even a shoe box). Whichever you choose, first cleanse and consecrate your chest by smudging it with sage smoke or incense and then splashing it with spring water mixed with a little sea salt. Next dedicate it to the hope of your choice.

You must then set about filling the hope chest. If you have a symbolic shoe box chest, you could write your hopes on slips of paper and add them as you think of them each day, keeping the chest on your altar. If you have a larger chest, you could fill it with items that represent your main goal. Say, for example, you've dedicated your hope chest to beginning a course of study, then you could fill it with paper, ring binders, study guides, pens and pencils, a pencil case – all the things you will need when you start studying. There are no limits to a hope chest – dedicate it to whatever you most want and gradually fill it. The more work you put into your hopes and dreams, the more likely they are to manifest.

August

Dawn 04.57
Dusk 19.10

Monday 21st

Moon quarter	4th (waning)	Herb or incense	Fennel
Moon sign	♋ 06.33 ♌	Crystal	Red Jasper
Colour	Gold	Sun sign	♌

Tuesday 22nd

Moon quarter	4th (waning)	Herb or incense	Dill
Moon sign	♌	Crystal	Amber
Colour	Red	Sun sign	♌

Wednesday 23rd

Moon phase	●	Colour	Purple
Time	19.10	Herb or incense	Valerian
Moon quarter	1st (waxing)	Crystal	Kunzite
Moon sign	♌ 07.01 ♍	Sun sign	♌ 06.23 ♍

Thursday 24th

Moon quarter	1st (waxing)	Herb or incense	Sage
Moon sign	♍	Crystal	Hematite
Colour	Indigo	Sun sign	♍

Friday 25th

Moon quarter	1st (waxing)	Herb or incense	Lavender
Moon sign	♍	Crystal	Topaz
Colour	Green	Sun sign	♍

Saturday 26th

Moon quarter	1st (waxing)	Herb or incense	Jasmine
Moon sign	♍ 07.01 ♎	Crystal	Sodalite
Colour	Grey	Sun sign	♍

Sunday 27th

Moon quarter	1st (waxing)	Crystal	Snowflake-Obsidian
Moon sign	♎	Sun sign	♍
Colour	Blue	Special	19.30 Mercury ☿ enters Virgo ♍
Herb or incense	Bay		

Dawn 05.07
Dusk 18.56

Monday 28th			
Moon quarter	1st (waxing)	Herb or incense	Mace
Moon sign	♎ 19.56 ♏	Crystal	Tiger's Eye
Colour	Orange	Sun sign	♍

Tuesday 29th			
Moon quarter	1st (waxing)	Herb or incense	Nutmeg
Moon sign	♏	Crystal	Aventurine
Colour	Brown	Sun sign	♍

Wednesday 30th			
Moon quarter	1st (waxing)	Herb or incense	Rosemary
Moon sign	♏	Crystal	Carnelian
Colour	Jade	Sun sign	♍

Thursday 31st			
Moon phase	◐	Colour	White
Time	22.56	Herb or incense	Thyme
Moon quarter	2nd (waxing)	Crystal	Citrine
Moon sign	♏07.00 ♐	Sun sign	♍

SUN MOVES INTO VIRGO

The sun now enters Virgo, which is symbolised by the virgin corn maiden, representing the harvest. Virgo is ruled by Mercury, the messenger, making those born under this sign very good communicators. The birthstone is the peridot, while the power stone is the beautiful crystal.

Virgos thrive on study and acquiring information. They are very concientious workers. However, this may lead to a kind of perfectionism others find infuriating! Virgos like to be surrounded with the familiar and can become a little nervous when faced with the unknown. At their best they are hard-working, logical, practical, modest and realistic, and they love to be of service to others. Definitely a rock to lean upon.

Autumn Leaves and Cobwebs

Autumn leaves and cobwebs,
A season of russet and gold,
When witches ride their broomsticks,
And Gypsy fortunes are told,

When ghosts walk in the swirling mists,
And vampires stalk their prey,
When bats fly through the woods at night,
And wolves at the moon do bay.

Cauldrons simmering bubbling brews,
The Wheel of the Year has turned.
As darkness falls and the veil thins,
We remember those who were burned.

Bonfires burning, circle-dance turning,
Witches who meet in the night,
Chestnuts are roasting, phantoms are haunting,
As the year turns away from the light.

As the boughs hang heavy with berries,
Mother Nature now takes her sleep;
We light our lives with candles,
And our magical goals we reap.

Leaves flutter to the forest floor,
As the trees stand black and bare;
Goblins and ghouls take their flight
At the sight of the pumpkin's glare.

And if you believe superstition,
'Tis the night when souls are sold,
And if you believe in the legends,
'Tis a night for the powers of old.

As the Wild Hunt rides and we call in the tides,
Crisp autumn leaves left to mould,
We cast spell, we work charm, but none do we harm
In this season of russet and gold.

September

September is a time of transition. The children go back to school and we know that the summer is over. The nights are beginning to draw in, and the sun, though still golden, has lost much of its power and strength. The first leaves fall from the trees, gusts of wind blow in the new season of autumn and we prepare for the dark time. This is also the month of the autumnal equinox, or Mabon as it is known among witches. I love September. For me it is the start of my favourite half of the year, the dark season. Autumn is so colourful, with the bright berries weighing down the hedgerows and leaves falling from the trees in a brilliant array of bronze, gold, russet, brown and red. Falling leaves, spring blossoms and winter snow flakes all seem to be different aspects of nature's own confetti! The world is still beautiful in its autumn colours, but we know that the silent sleep of winter is just around the corner and will soon be upon us.

The ancient Celts associated the ivy, or gort, with the month of September. Ivy is a very protective plant, and the tradition of growing it up the side of a building is a way of invoking that protection. Ivy is also a binding plant and so is used in spells of this type. It is extremely hardy and will flourish in almost any condition, dark or light, damp or dry. Once ivy takes a hold of something it is almost impossible to get rid of, and so it is a symbol of great resilience. Ivy is a beautiful plant with very pretty leaves, and at one time it was brought into the house during the darker months as a magical way of keeping 'greens' in the cupboard and thus saving the family from starvation or malnutrition. Ivy can be grown indoors in pots, or you might like to plant some in your garden or by the side of your house. Magically speaking, it can help us to connect with our higher self and will teach us to listen to our inner voice, so it is a great plant to choose for your ritual space. It is also an appropriate plant for your Green Man shrine.

September

The protective quality of ivy is echoed in this month's flower, the gladioli, which also stands for protection. You can plant gladioli in a pot by your front door to make the most of their powers, or maybe keep them by your garden gate. In contrast, the herbs of the month are the shy violet and the wild rose, or dog rose as it is also known. Keeping a little violet plant in your room may help you to be more confident. Adding violet essential oil to your bath water may have the same effect. The seasonal gift of the wild rose is the rose hip, so bring a few indoors to adorn your altar, or use rose hip wine as your ritual tipple and libation.

Dawn 05.07
Dusk 18.56

Friday 1st			
Moon quarter	2nd (waxing)	Herb or incense	Valerian
Moon sign	♐	Crystal	Bloodstone
Colour	Red	Sun sign	♍

Saturday 2nd			
Moon quarter	2nd (waxing)	Herb or incense	Fennel
Moon sign	♐ 14.34 ♑	Crystal	Amethyst
Colour	Brown	Sun sign	♍

Sunday 3rd			
Moon quarter	2nd (waxing)	Herb or incense	Pine
Moon sign	♑	Crystal	Moonstone
Colour	Green	Sun sign	♍

Autumnal Pot Pourri

This is a fabulous way to bring the spirit of autumn into your altar room. You will need to get out into nature, taking with you a box or a bag to hold your finds. Go to a nice woodland area and ask the Green Man to furnish you with lots of autumn gifts. Now walk through the woods, collecting nature's spoils as you go. Fill your bag with autumn leaves of various hues, shades and shapes; fallen twigs and pieces of fallen bark; acorns and conkers; pine cones; seed pods and so on. Once you feel you have enough, take them home, giving thanks to nature and the Green Man.

Find a container large enough to hold all your finds – a pretty bowl, or a rustic-looking country basket. If you're using a basket, first line it with felt of an autumn colour. This will prevent all the bits and pieces from falling out between the basket weave. Now begin to arrange your collection, creating a pretty pot pourri. For the fragrance add slices of dried apple and orange, cloves or a few bundles of cinnamon sticks. Finally, splash the mixture with an essential oil of a woodland fragrance. You might choose pine, bramble, blackberry or apple, but my favourite oils for this purpose are rosewood and cedarwood, both very woody scents that, when mingled with the spoils of nature, truly evoke the fragrance of autumn.

Place your pot pourri on or near your altar or Green Man shrine. You may enjoy this project so much that you decide to fill your entire home with such seasonal mixtures – it's a good way to get the children out and about too! Another way to use autumn leaves in your magic is to fix them into your Book of Shadows, writing down the attributes of the tree and where it can be found in your area.

September

Dawn 05.18
Dusk 18.41

Monday 4th			
Moon quarter	2nd (waxing)	Herb or incense	Borage
Moon sign	♑ 18.15 ♒	Crystal	Opal
Colour	Blue	Sun sign	♍

Tuesday 5th			
Moon quarter	2nd (waxing)	Herb or incense	Lavender
Moon sign	♒	Crystal	Red Jasper
Colour	Yellow	Sun sign	♍

Wednesday 6th			
Moon quarter	2nd (waxing)	Crystal	Smokey Quartz
Moon sign	♒ 18.56 ♓	Sun sign	♍
Colour	Silver	Special	06.15 Venus ♀ enters Virgo ♍
Herb or incense	Angelica		

Thursday 7th			
Moon phase	○	Herb or incense	Jasmine
Time	18.42	Crystal	Rose Quartz
Moon quarter	3rd (waning)	Sun sign	♍
Moon sign	♓	Special	Barley Moon ☾ partial eclipse
Colour	Purple		

Friday 8th			
Moon quarter	3rd (waning)	Crystal	Tiger's Eye
Moon sign	♓ 18.23 ♈	Sun sign	♍
Colour	Peach	Special	04.18 Mars ♂ enters Libra ♎
Herb or incense	Rosemary		

Saturday 9th			
Moon quarter	3rd (waning)	Herb or incense	Mace
Moon sign	♈	Crystal	Hematite
Colour	Indigo	Sun sign	♍

Sunday 10th			
Moon quarter	3rd (waning)	Herb or incense	Mint
Moon sign	♈ 18.30 ♉	Crystal	Aventurine
Colour	Black	Sun sign	♍

BARLEY MOON

The traditional name for the full moon of September is the barley moon. You can incorporate this into your esbat rite by holding your power hand over a chalice of barley water and empowering it with a positive goal. Drink this potion as part of your ritual.

Autumn Fruits Warming Potion

This is a fabulous hot punch that can be enjoyed all through the months of autumn and winter. It's a great addition to any winter sabbat or gathering – and it does have quite a kick!

What you need: a large pan, 1 litre/1¾ pints cider, 500 ml/1 scant pint blackcurrant squash, a bottle of white wine, two generous glasses of sherry, two glasses of Martini Bianco, 3 tsp golden honey, two slices of apple, two slices of orange, two cinnamon sticks

- Pour the cider, blackcurrant squash, white wine, sherry and Martini Bianco into the pan. Gently warm the mixture on a low heat, stirring in the honey. Do not boil.
- Add the apple, orange and cinnamon sticks. Simmer for around 20 minutes and then fish out the fruit and cinnamon sticks.
- Serve the punch hot and enjoy!

Ginger Glow Potion (Alcohol-free)

What you need: a large pan, 2 litres/3½ pints ginger beer/ale, 500 ml/1 scant pint blackcurrant squash, 500 ml/1 scant pint red grape juice, 3 tsp golden honey, two slices apple, two slices orange, two cinnamon sticks, a piece of ginger root

- Pour the ginger beer/ale, blackcurrant squash and red grape juice into the pan. Simmer gently, stirring in the honey.
- Add the apple, orange, cinnamon and ginger root, and simmer for about 20 minutes.
- Fish out the ginger, cinnamon and fruit, and serve hot.

September

Dawn 05.28 Dusk 18.26

Monday 11th			
Moon quarter	3rd (waning)	Crystal	Bloodstone
Moon sign	♉	Sun sign	♍
Colour	Yellow	Special	World Trade Center
Herb or incense	Pine		Remembrance Day

Tuesday 12th			
Moon quarter	3rd (waning)	Crystal	Moonstone
Moon sign	♉ 20.59 ♊	Sun sign	♍
Colour	Blue	Special	21.08 Mercury ☿
Herb or incense	Mugwort		enters Libra ♎

Wednesday 13th			
Moon quarter	3rd (waning)	Herb or incense	Cinnamon
Moon sign	♊	Crystal	Carnelian
Colour	Orange	Sun sign	♍

Thursday 14th			
Moon phase	◑	Colour	Grey
Time	11.15	Herb or incense	Bayberry
Moon quarter	4th (waning)	Crystal	Topaz
Moon sign	♊	Sun sign	♍

Friday 15th			
Moon quarter	4th (waning)	Herb or incense	Catnip
Moon sign	♊ 02.53 ♋	Crystal	Jasper
Colour	Pink	Sun sign	♍

Saturday 16th			
Moon quarter	4th (waning)	Herb or incense	Borage
Moon sign	♋	Crystal	Kunzite
Colour	Silver	Sun sign	♍

Sunday 17th			
Moon quarter	4th (waning)	Herb or incense	Parsley
Moon sign	♋ 12.15 ♌	Crystal	Amber
Colour	Red	Sun sign	♍

Healing Love Ritual 11 September

The terrorist attack on the twin towers of New York's World Trade Center in September 2001 shook our planet to the core. Thousands of innocent lives were lost, and the world listened numbly to the recorded messages left by those who didn't return home that day.

Disasters and tragedies do happen. No one can explain them, no one can justify them, and although we are often limited in what we can do to help, we can at least magically send our healing blessings to those in need. Love knows no limits, no boundaries.

Purpose of ritual: to send healing love and blessings to those afflicted by tragedy

What you need: an angel lantern or representation of an angel, lavender essential oil, a tea-light and holder

- Take the angel representation to your altar. Close your eyes and call on your guardian angel and the angels of healing and love for assistance. Wait until you feel a state of calm wash over you – this is the arrival of angel power.
- Place one drop of lavender essential oil on to the tea-light and place this in the lantern or holder. If you are using a holder, place it in front of the angel representation.
- Light the tea-light and say these words or similar as you hold your hands out to the candle light:

By fire, by spell, by angel power,
I send out my love at this tragic hour.
Love travel lightly, healing be swift;
Angels I ask you to carry forth my gift.
With love and bright blessings, these words I do speak
To heal those afflicted and give strength to the weak.
With magic and with witchcraft I send forth my love,
Carried with a blessing, on the wings of a dove.
So mote it be!

- When you have asked the angels to carry love and healing to those in need, let the tea-light burn down. Repeat the ritual daily until there is no longer any need.

SUN MOVES INTO LIBRA

On September 23rd the sun enters Libra, a sign symbolised by the scales. Libra's power stone is the pyrite (also known as fool's gold), and the birthstone for those born under this sign is the sapphire. Libra is ruled by Venus, planet of love, and most Librans are peace-loving, nurturing people. As the scales suggest, they like to keep a sense of balance in their lives, and should the scales tip too far one way or the other, they can begin to feel insecure.

Librans can sometimes find themselves saying things they don't mean simply to keep the peace. It's anything for a quiet life with these guys! This can sometimes come across as insincerity, but at their most positive Librans are fair, just, diplomatic and trustworthy.

Balancing Spell

As Mabon is the season of balance, we are going to work towards putting a little balance into our lives.

Purpose of ritual: to bring balance into your life
What you need: two pebbles or crystals, one light in colour, the other dark; your pentacle; two small slips of paper; a black pen; a gold or silver pen

- Place the pebbles on your altar, on top of your pentacle, to charge.
- Think of something you'd like to reduce in your life and something you'd like to increase, such as working less and spending more time with the kids. The two aspects don't have to be relative to one another, and you should try to get to the root of what you need. For example, don't choose stress, look for what is causing your stress.
- Write the things you want to decrease on one of the slips of paper, using the black pen, and the things you want to increase on the other, using the gold or silver pen.
- Fold the slips in half and place them at either far side of your altar. Place the dark pebble on the decrease slip and the light pebble on the increase one.
- Leave the slips of paper in place for three days, then burn both of them and bury the dark pebble in the earth, keeping the lighter one on your altar.

September

Dawn 05.38
Dusk 18.10

Monday 18th			
Moon quarter	4th (waning)	Herb or incense	Valerian
Moon sign	♌	Crystal	Moonstone
Colour	Purple	Sun sign	♍

Tuesday 19th			
Moon quarter	4th (waning)	Herb or incense	Fennel
Moon sign	♌	Crystal	Amber
Colour	Blue	Sun sign	♍

Wednesday 20th			
Moon quarter	4th (waning)	Crystal	Rose Quartz
Moon sign	♌ 00.07 ♍	Sun sign	♍
Colour	Gold	Special	International Day of Peace
Herb or incense	Jasmine		☾ annular eclipse

Thursday 21st			
Moon quarter	4th (waning)	Herb or incense	Bay
Moon sign	♍	Crystal	Amethyst
Colour	Brown	Sun sign	♍

Friday 22nd			
Moon phase	●	Colour	Gold
Time	11.45	Herb or incense	Pine
Moon quarter	1st (waxing)	Crystal	Hematite
Moon sign	♍ 13.06 ♎	Sun sign	♍

Saturday 23rd			
Moon quarter	1st (waxing)	Crystal	Amber
Moon sign	♎	Sun sign	♍ 04.03 ♎
Colour	Peach	Special	Mabon (04.03)
Herb or incense	Mint		

Sunday 24th			
Moon quarter	1st (waxing)	Herb or incense	Catnip
Moon sign	♎	Crystal	Citrine
Colour	Green	Sun sign	♎

MABON

Mabon is the sabbat of the autumnal equinox. It is named after the Welsh god of the same name and is the second harvest festival. It is a time of balance, when once again the hours of dark and light are equal. From now on the dark will strengthen its grip on the world. The days will become shorter, the nights longer and longer. This is a time when magic is worked for protection and also for balance in our lives. It is also a time of thanksgiving for all we have and all we enjoy.

Your altar should be covered with a brown or bronze cloth and sprinkled with autumn leaves. Two brown or russet candles should be placed in appropriate holders, or you might like to put tea-lights in leaf-shaped holders. It's also possible to get hold of leaf-shaped floating candles, which you might like to include in your altar set-up. Add a bowl of Autumnal Pot Pourri (see page 167) and a plate of berries and rose hips, and fill your decanter with bramble, oak leaf or elderberry wine, and your altar will be the spirit of autumn.

Mabon is the season sacred to Persephone, so her fruit, the pomegranate, would also be appropriate, as would any representation of her. Over my altar I have a large print of Persephone by the Pre-Raphaelite artist Dante Gabriel Rossetti. Such prints are widely available, particularly as postcards, so you can obtain one quite cheaply if you like the idea.

Seasonal incenses include cinnamon, ginger, nutmeg, apple, blackberry and pine. If you would really like to bring the fragrance of autumn to your ritual space, there is a wide range of synthetic oils available. These should not be used as spell ingredients under any circumstances, but you can burn them in an oil burner (the only purpose they are intended for) to evoke the spirit of the season. They come with such enticing names as Autumn Fall, Winter Frost, Autumn Berries, Fallen Leaves and Blackberry Musk. They can be a lovely atmospheric addition to ritual and to your altar room.

A walk in the woods, reflection on the Green Man or reading the myths of the goddess Persephone could all play a part in your celebrations, as could working on your nature notebook or Book of Shadows. Your ritual feast should include stews and soups, breads, pomegranates, apples, apple pies, berry pies, gingerbread and ginger cakes, chocolate leaves, rum truffles and the Autumn Potions for which recipes are given on page 169.

Persephone Protection Spell

As this is the time of Persephone, we can call on her assistance with our protection magic. Persephone is Queen of the Underworld, and she rules over the dark season. Her fruit, as already mentioned, is the pomegranate.

Purpose of ritual: to call on Persephone for protection
What you need: two pomegranates, a knife, your pentacle

- Take the pomegranates to your altar and light the candles, calling on the powers of Persephone.
- Cut each fruit in two, giving you four halves. Place these on your pentacle to charge.
- Nine is a number sacred to the Goddess so repeat the following charm nine times:

Sweet Persephone, enchantress, queen,
Protect me from harm, seen and unseen.
Protect me from theft, fire and flood;
Protect me from those who mean no good.
Keep me safe in your season of dusk;
Grant me the wisdom to know who to trust.
Protect me at work, protect me at home;
Keep safe my abode of earth, wood and stone.
I bury your fruit in the depths of earth's womb;
Weave now my safety at the magical loom.
So be it!

- Extinguish the candles and bury the pomegranate halves at the four corners of your property.

September

Dawn 05.49
Dusk 17.55

Monday 25th			
Moon quarter	1st (waxing)	Herb or incense	Borage
Moon sign	♎ 01.54 ♏	Crystal	Moonstone
Colour	Pink	Sun sign	♎

Tuesday 26th			
Moon quarter	1st (waxing)	Herb or incense	Lavender
Moon sign	♏	Crystal	Red Jasper
Colour	Blue	Sun sign	♎

Wednesday 27th			
Moon quarter	1st (waxing)	Herb or incense	Angelica
Moon sign	♏ 13.16 ♐	Crystal	Opal
Colour	Grey	Sun sign	♎

Thursday 28th			
Moon quarter	1st (waxing)	Herb or incense	Thyme
Moon sign	♐	Crystal	Amber
Colour	Silver	Sun sign	♎

Friday 29th			
Moon quarter	1st (waxing)	Herb or incense	Sage
Moon sign	♐ 22.01 ♑	Crystal	Aventurine
Colour	White	Sun sign	♎

Saturday 30th			
Moon phase	◐	Herb or incense	Parsley
Time	11.04	Crystal	Carnelian
Moon quarter	2nd (waxing)	Sun sign	♎
Moon sign	♑	Special	10.02 Venus ♀ enters Libra ♎
Colour	Blue		

Spell for Plentiful Food

In times past, winter starvation was a serious threat. The very old and the very young were at particular risk, and so magic was worked to keep hunger at bay during the darker months. These days most of us don't have to worry about such things. But even so there are those who remain vulnerable.

This little spell uses a cornucopia, or horn of plenty (a horn-shaped woven basket), to symbolise plenty for all.

Purpose of spell:	to ensure that winter is a time of plenty
What you need:	a cornucopia – obtainable from most flower stores and craft shops, an essential oil of your choice, a small tea-light and holder, a jar of salt, a small green plant (ivy is particularly appropriate), some dried foods such as nuts and seeds (optional)

- Take the cornucopia to your altar and anoint it with the oil.
- Hold it in your hands and visualise yourself and your family having all that you need through the winter months. Imagine scenes of abundance: Yuletide tables laden with food; bowls piled high with fruit, nuts and berries; large joints of meat roasting in the oven and filling your home with a delicious scent; cupboards full of canned goods; a freezer filled with ice-cream and out-of-season luxuries such as strawberries; a wine rack stacked with bottles of deep red burgundy; pots of simmering stews, soups and so on.
- Now turn your attention to other practicalities and focus on a steady income throughout the winter, maybe some healthy savings, a home filled with heat and light, a reliable car that gets you where you need to go in spite of winter weather and so on.
- Once you have finished your visualisation, take the cornucopia to the kitchen and place it on the window sill. If you are using dried foods, fill the cornucopia with them – this will help to reaffirm your state of abundance.
- Next to the cornucopia, place the tea-light, the salt (which represents money and finances) and the plant (to keep greens in your diet).
- Light the tea-light and say these words:

The world is full of abundance. I accept abundance in my life.
I accept good things to eat and drink. I accept a regular
income and a home filled with light and warmth throughout
the dark seasons of autumn and winter. So mote it be!

- Allow your tea-light to burn down and light another every day as you prepare your evening meal. Keep your little space clean and clutter-free, and tend the plant with care. You may like this space so much that you decide to keep it all year round, but make sure that you renew the spell every autumn to keep the magic working.

Blessing for a Departed Spirit

Spirit fly, spirit soar,
Sorrow and pain you'll know no more.
Spirit soar, spirit fly,
Farewell only – never goodbye.

As above, so below;
Your love for us will burn and glow,
And light the way for all to see.
Go with our love. Blessed be!

Hear these words, hear my cry,
Spirits on the other side.
Hail and welcome now another,
Who comes to rest in the arms of the Mother.

October

The October evening sun glows a deep burnt orange, like a pumpkin on the horizon, reflected in autumn puddles. The trees are a blaze of colour, their dried golden leaves rustling as the chill wind passes through the branches. A solitary fox searches the suburban streets for food. The longer nights mean that nocturnal animals are more active; the dark hours belong to the owl, the bat and creatures like them. This is the month of swirling mists and damp fogs, heavy showers and the wonderful tang of fresh fallen leaves in the air. The magical veil between our world and the Otherworld is thinning and will be at its thinnest on October 31st, the sabbat of Samhain, the night of the witches. Shadows in the twilight, the glow of a cat's eyes, the cries of wild animals in the dark all add to the almost eerie atmosphere of October. The world is becoming still and quiet; the Earth is ready for slumber and rest. This is a most magical time.

To the Celts, October was linked with the elder tree, or ruis. In the old Celtic calendar, October was actually the last month of the year, which is why Samhain is still known to witches as New Year. Thus the elder tree is symbolic of beginnings and endings entwined, or death and rebirth. In Wiccan belief the elder is sacred to the Goddess in her third aspect, the Crone.

Elderberry wine is considered a suitable drink for ritual and to offer in libation at the waning and dark moon – the Dark Goddess's prominent time. The Wiccan Rede states that:

Elder be ye Lady's tree,
Burn it not or cursed ye'll be!

There is a very practical reason behind this statement, in that elder spits and jumps when heated, so it really isn't a safe wood to burn!

The flower of October is the aster, which is symbolic of truth. To find out the truth of a situation from someone, give them an aster flower that has been empowered to your purpose. The herbs of the month are ginger, cinnamon and basil, and these are excellent to burn as incense during ritual and spells.

Magically speaking, October is a time for releasing negative emotions and habits, communing with the Dark Goddess and accepting her wisdom, and communicating with loved ones who have passed over – though this does not mean summoning spirits and table-tapping games. Witches have respect for the dead and there are better ways of honouring them.

Sunday 1st

Dawn 05.49 Dusk 17.55

Moon quarter	2nd (waxing)	Herb or incense	Jasmine
Moon sign	♑	Crystal	Citrine
Colour	Brown	Sun sign	♎

Owl Magic

Owl magic is another form of divination that has roots deep in folk magic. Go to a wooded area where you know owls live. Focus intently upon your question and then speak it aloud to the wise old owls. Listen carefully for the reply. If you hear an owl hoot once, then your answer is positive; if it hoots twice the answer is negative, and you might want to alter your present course. If the owl hoots repeatedly, the outcome is unclear and you should ask your question again at a later date.

Pumpkin Seed Divination

Divination, or fortune-telling, is a traditional practice at this time of year, and could be performed as part of your Samhain ritual. This particular divination uses a very seasonal tool – pumpkin seeds.

What you need: 13 pumpkin seeds; a small pouch; model paint or nail polish in each of the following colours: clear, black, grey, bright red, deep red, green, blue, yellow, pink, orange, purple, gold and silver

- Wash the pumpkin seeds in warm soapy water and allow them to dry.
- Once the seeds have dried thoroughly, paint each one a different colour, using the list above. Allow the painted seeds to dry and then transfer them to the pouch.
- To use the seeds, ponder your question clearly, shake the pouch and draw out up to three seeds. Use the interpretations below to divine your answer:

Clear: a positive answer; you are on the right path.
Black: a negative answer; tough times ahead; you might like to change your course.
Grey: neutrality; the future is unclear; ask again later.
Bright red: love, passion, excitement; your instincts are good, so follow your heart.
Deep red: danger ahead; deception and deceit; a lesson learned.
Green: Earth magic, security, prosperity, fertility, general growth; a good sign.
Blue: a time of calmness and healing, harmony and tranquillity; a period of rest.
Yellow: intellect; think things through logically; take one step at a time.
Pink: friendships, new love, new acquaintances, self-love; take care of your own needs.
Orange: communication, social events, happiness, party time!
Purple: introspection, dreams, psychic abilities and awareness, magic, meditation; listen to your intuition.
Gold: masculinity, the sun, daylight hours, productivity; draw on inner strength; God energy, protection.
Silver: femininity, the moon, night, creativity; surround yourself with magical power; Goddess energy, protection.

October

Dawn 06.00
Dusk 17.40

Monday 2nd			
Moon quarter	2nd (waxing)	Crystal	Snowflake-Obsidian
Moon sign	♑ 03.24 ♒	Sun sign	♎
Colour	Gold	Special	04.38 Mercury ☿ enters Scorpio ♏
Herb or incense	Bay		

Tuesday 3rd			
Moon quarter	2nd (waxing)	Herb or incense	Lavender
Moon sign	♒	Crystal	Kunzite
Colour	Orange	Sun sign	♎

Wednesday 4th			
Moon quarter	2nd (waxing)	Herb or incense	Sage
Moon sign	♒ 05.33 ♓	Crystal	Topaz
Colour	Grey	Sun sign	♎

Thursday 5th			
Moon quarter	2nd (waxing)	Herb or incense	Mace
Moon sign	♓	Crystal	Red Jasper
Colour	White	Sun sign	♎

Friday 6th			
Moon quarter	2nd (waxing)	Herb or incense	Dill
Moon sign	♓ 05.32 ♈	Crystal	Opal
Colour	Pink	Sun sign	♎

Saturday 7th			
Moon phase	○	Herb or incense	Angelica
Time	03.13	Crystal	Moonstone
Moon quarter	3rd (waning)	Sun sign	♎
Moon sign	♈	Special	Blood Moon
Colour	Blue		

Sunday 8th			
Moon quarter	3rd (waning)	Herb or incense	Rosemary
Moon sign	♈ 05.04 ♉	Crystal	Carnelian
Colour	Silver	Sun sign	♎

BLOOD MOON

The full moon of October is known among witches as the blood moon. A chalice of deep red wine can be used to symbolise this in ritual.

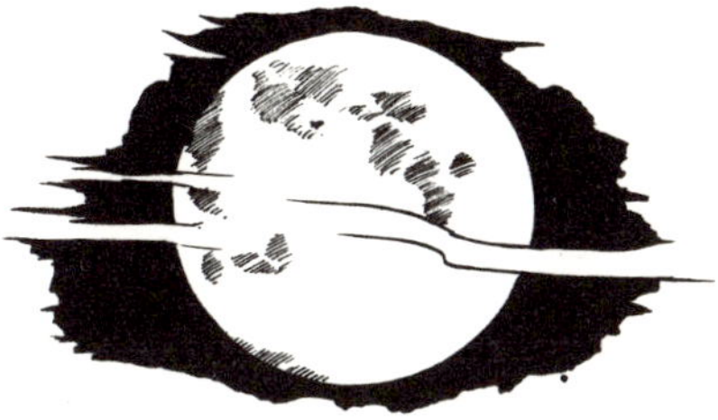

Falling Leaf Banishing Spell

As the old moon begins to wane, now is the perfect time for a gentle banishing spell to remove something from your life. This could be a bad habit, an outdated mode of thinking or an attitude.

To do this spell you will need to be in a place where you have a clear view of a tree that is shedding its leaves. If you can see such a tree from inside your house, fine. If not, work the spell outside.

Purpose of ritual: to remove something unwanted from your life

- Standing where you can clearly see your tree, silently call on its dryad, or protective guardian, and explain that you require this elemental's assistance in your magic.
- Concentrate on the negative aspect of your life that you wish to release. Imagine how it will feel to be free of it and how your life will improve when it has gone. Keep focusing on banishing this particular aspect of negativity and then slowly and steadily begin to chant the following charm:

  As the next leaf falls from this tree,
  It takes ------- away from me.

- Wait until you see a leaf fall – you may even notice a shower of leaves – and know that your magic is now in progress. Back up your spell in the mundane world and your banishing will be successful.

Ancestral Protection

Our ancestors can provide powerful protection. This advanced ritual has a very strong magical working and should be used only if you feel threatened.

Be aware that this spell will leave you feeling quite drained, as it takes a lot of energy and focus. Eat and drink something immediately after performing the rite and relax for the remainder of the day, knowing that you are safe. Also, don't be surprised if the appliances in your house begin to go awry because of the vast amounts of energy you have summoned. When I cast this spell a couple of years ago, calling the ancient Bruce clansmen, the light bulbs blew, the microwave and hoover fused, the fridge-freezer broke down and the video packed up!

Purpose of ritual: to seek protection from your ancestors
What you need: candles for the quarters (optional), incense (optional)

- Cast the Circle and call the angelic quarters. Light quarter candles and incense if you wish.
- Raise your arms high in invocation and strongly visualise how your ancestors would have looked.
- Now ask them to come in the following way:

I,------(state your full name), daughter/son of the line of
-------(state your family/maiden name) do call on my
ancient ancestors in honour and respect.
I call all ancestors who wish to help and aid me, all ancestors
who will work for my highest good.
I call you here now into my sacred space.
Ancient clansmen/Vikings (or whatever) of my bloodline,
I stir thee and call thee forth, and I ask for your protection.
Ancestors, guard me and protect me from all who would do
me harm. Shield me from hurt and pain, and protect me until
I am safe to release you.
So mote it be!

- You may feel a strong energy in the Circle and you should release this immediately by taking the Circle down, so that your ancestors can do the job you've called them to do.
- There is no need to repeat this spell, but once the danger has passed you must cast the Circle again and release your ancestors from their duty, giving thanks.

October

Dawn 06.10
Dusk 17.25

Monday 9th

Moon quarter	3rd (waning)	Herb or incense	Parsley
Moon sign	♉	Crystal	Aventurine
Colour	Peach	Sun sign	♎

Tuesday 10th

Moon quarter	3rd (waning)	Herb or incense	Mugwort
Moon sign	♉ 06.06 ♊	Crystal	Hematite
Colour	Indigo	Sun sign	♎

Wednesday 11th

Moon quarter	3rd (waning)	Herb or incense	Valerian
Moon sign	♊	Crystal	Bloodstone
Colour	Purple	Sun sign	♎

Thursday 12th

Moon quarter	3rd (waning)	Herb or incense	Borage
Moon sign	♊ 10.21 ♋	Crystal	Jasper
Colour	Jade	Sun sign	♎

Friday 13th

Moon quarter	3rd (waning)	Herb or incense	Jasmine
Moon sign	♋	Crystal	Amber
Colour	Orange	Sun sign	♎

Saturday 14th

Moon phase	◑	Colour	Black
Time	00.26	Herb or incense	Catnip
Moon quarter	4th (waning)	Crystal	Sodalite
Moon sign	♋ 18.38 ♌	Sun sign	♎

Sunday 15th

Moon quarter	4th (waning)	Herb or incense	Bayberry
Moon sign	♌	Crystal	Topaz
Colour	Pink	Sun sign	♎

October

Dawn 06.22
Dusk 17.10

Monday 16th			
Moon quarter	4th (waning)	Herb or incense	Mint
Moon sign	♌	Crystal	Tiger's Eye
Colour	Blue	Sun sign	♎

Tuesday 17th			
Moon quarter	4th (waning)	Herb or incense	Cinnamon
Moon sign	♌ 06.16 ♍	Crystal	Rose Quartz
Colour	Yellow	Sun sign	♎

Wednesday 18th			
Moon quarter	4th (waning)	Herb or incense	Fennel
Moon sign	♍	Crystal	Obsidian
Colour	Green	Sun sign	♎

Thursday 19th			
Moon quarter	4th (waning)	Herb or incense	Lavender
Moon sign	♍ 19.19 ♎	Crystal	Amber
Colour	Pink	Sun sign	♎

Friday 20th			
Moon quarter	4th (waning)	Herb or incense	Nutmeg
Moon sign	♎	Crystal	Kunzite
Colour	Red	Sun sign	♎

Saturday 21st			
Moon quarter	4th (waning)	Herb or incense	Jasmine
Moon sign	♎	Crystal	Citrine
Colour	Brown	Sun sign	♎

Sunday 22nd			
Moon phase	●	Colour	Purple
Time	05.14	Herb or incense	Cinnamon
Moon quarter	1st (waxing)	Crystal	Aventurine
Moon sign	♎ 07.54 ♏	Sun sign	♎ 13.26 ♏

SUN MOVES INTO SCORPIO

On October 22nd, the sun enters Scorpio. The power stone for this sign is the opal, while the birth stone is the lovely blue topaz. Scorpio's ruling planet is Pluto. In mythology, Pluto was the god of the Underworld, the Dark Lord, and Scorpios certainly do have a dark side! Their key words are power and control – they like to be in charge and don't take any nonsense from anyone!

Scorpio is probably the most complex sign in the zodiac, and those born under it can often be misunderstood, but let's not beat around the bush here: Scorpios have a definite underlying streak of ruthlessness. They can be cold, calculating, suspicious, jealous and very manipulative. But they do have their good side! Loyal to their loved ones, decisive in their nature, passionate in love and romance, and very independent, they have an aura of strength and mystery. Known for being the sexiest people in the zodiac and for bearing a sting in the tail that they're not afraid to use, Scorpios can summon up their tremendous courage at the drop of a hat.

Banishing Incense

This powder can be burnt as an incense in small amounts on a charcoal block (though it smells pretty gross). Alternatively, it can be scattered around the magic Circle or your home, used in candle magic or spell pouches, and even sprinkled (discreetly) on the shoes of someone you want to get rid of! – with harm to none, of course.

What you need: a mortar and pestle, 1 tsp dried basil, 1 tsp black pepper, 1 tsp garlic powder, 1 tsp holy thistle, a charcoal stick (available from art stores), an airtight jar, a label

- In the mortar and pestle, grind together the basil, black pepper, garlic powder, holy thistle and charcoal stick thoroughly, using a widdershins (or anti-clockwise) motion. This is the direction of all banishing magic.
- When you have a fine powder, transfer the mixture to an airtight jar and label it appropriately.

October

Dawn 06.33
Dusk 16.56

Monday 23rd

Moon quarter	1st (waxing)	Crystal	Smokey Quartz
Moon sign	♏	Sun sign	♏
Colour	Pink	Special	16.38 Mars ♂ enters Scorpio ♏
Herb or incense	Valerian		

Tuesday 24th

Moon quarter	1st (waxing)	Sun sign	♏
Moon sign	♏ 18.53 ♐	Special	United Nations' Day 09.58 Venus ♀ enters Scorpio ♏
Colour	Blue		
Herb or incense	Angelica		
Crystal	Snowflake-Obsidian		

Wednesday 25th

Moon quarter	1st (waxing)	Herb or incense	Thyme
Moon sign	♐	Crystal	Bloodstone
Colour	Green	Sun sign	♏

Thursday 26th

Moon quarter	1st (waxing)	Herb or incense	Borage
Moon sign	♐	Crystal	Tiger's Eye
Colour	Yellow	Sun sign	♏

Friday 27th

Moon quarter	1st (waxing)	Herb or incense	Mace
Moon sign	♐ 03.47 ♑	Crystal	Aventurine
Colour	Jade	Sun sign	♏

Saturday 28th

Moon quarter	1st (waxing)	Herb or incense	Catnip
Moon sign	♑	Crystal	Sodalite
Colour	Indigo	Sun sign	♏

Sunday 29th

Moon phase	◐	Herb or incense	Valerian
Time	21.25	Crystal	Carnelian
Moon quarter	2nd (waxing)	Sun sign	♏
Moon sign	♑ 10.17 ♒	Special	British Summer Time ends
Colour	Gold		

Monday 30th			
Moon quarter	2nd (waxing)	Herb or incense	Fennel
Moon sign	♒	Crystal	Carnelian
Colour	Black	Sun sign	♏

Dawn 06.44
Dusk 16.43

Tuesday 31st			
Moon quarter	2nd (waxing)	Crystal	Kunzite
Moon sign	♒ 03.24 ♓	Sun sign	♏
Colour	Orange	Special	Samhain
Herb or incense	Mugwort		

Spell for a Lost Love

Whether the pain comes from the break-up of a long-term relationship or from an unrequited love, it can leave us feeling empty inside. This ritual is designed to help you get back on your feet. Don't perform it immediately after the break-up or romantic disappointment, as you will need time to heal. You will know when the time is right to do this spell.

Purpose of spell: to heal yourself after a love has been lost
What you need: a mirror, a deep pink pillar candle and a holder, an essential oil of your choice

- Sit before the mirror and anoint the candle with the essential oil. Place it in the holder and light the wick. No other light or candle should be on in the room; you should see only the light of your spell candle reflected in the mirror before you.
- Gaze into the depths of your own eyes in the mirror and chant:

We've all loved,
We've all lost,
We've all felt the pain.
Pick yourself up,
Dust yourself off,
Get back in the game.

- Keep chanting for as long as you comfortably can, then blow out the candle, keeping it to repeat the spell again as often as you need. It's worth noting that the game in the spell is the game of life rather than the game of love, so even if you don't feel ready to try again with someone new, you can still use the spell to help you move on in your life and to assist with the healing process.

SAMHAIN

Glowing pumpkins, flickering candles, bubbling cauldrons, spirit boards and Wicca gatherings ... it's the festival of Samhain (pronounced Sow-een), the night of the witches and probably our most important sabbat. Any of the spells in the October and November months can be used as a part of your celebrations, and remember that the sabbat runs from sunset to sunset, so you have all day tomorrow to celebrate too – maybe you can even enjoy two ritual feasts!

Samhain (meaning 'summer's end' and known to non-witches as Halloween) is one of my favourite sabbats. I really love the dark season and all that it brings. I get out my more subtle Samhain decorations at the beginning of October to remind me that the seasons are changing and the darkness is coming into its own. To me, the altar set-ups of Samhain and Yule are the nicest of the whole year.

A Samhain altar should be covered with a black cloth. Add a couple of black candles and, of course, a carved pumpkin lantern and you have a basic altar. However, there are many other things you might choose to add. I have a collection of ceramic tea-light holders shaped like pumpkins, and a couple of little witch candle holders – the tea-light is meant to represent the ritual bonfire! In September and October you can also buy candles and tea-light holders fashioned to look like pumpkins, ghosts, skulls, vampires, haunted houses, black cats and, of course, witches. Make your altar as serious or as fun as you like – it's your ritual after all. Figures of the stereotypical witch abound at this time and you can add these to your altar to represent the Crone, or Dark Goddess. Alternatively, you could use figures of snakes or black cats, or maybe statues of ravens and crows to represent the Morrigan.

Samhain fragrances include patchouli, Night Queen, ginger and cinnamon. You might even like to buy the scented candles produced for Halloween and fragranced with 'pumpkin' and 'witch's brew'!

For your ritual feast you are spoilt for choice. Walk into any bakery and you will find bats, cats, witches and pumpkins made from gingerbread; ghosts and gouls made from meringues; and little sponge cakes with vampires on top. Add to these chocolate pumpkins, chocolate frogs, jelly snakes and so on, and you will soon be getting into the swing of things! On a more adult level, you could indulge in roasted chestnuts, pomegranates, pumpkin pie, hot dogs, casseroles, flapjacks, parkin, jacket potatoes and a hot autumn punch.

Gather your friends together or celebrate alone, it doesn't matter. Perform the magic and ritual of your choice, and end the festival with a scary movie or a horror novel, or study your Wicca books. Work on your Book of Shadows, take a midnight walk, burn spell papers to release old habits and negative influences, work with your totem animal, and don't forget to finish off your ritual with a feast.

To Commune with the Dead

As I have mentioned, October and November are the months when the veil between the worlds is thinning, so sightings of ghosts and unexplained phenomena are more frequent. Witches make the most of this powerful time to communicate with their dear departed.

This ritual is best done last thing at night. While you are performing it, be aware of any sign of your loved one: a familiar scent, the flicker of a light bulb, a jump in the CD, a guttering candle. If nothing happens, don't despair – sometimes it can take a while for our messages to get through. Your loved one may come to you in a dream within the next few nights, or the radio may play their favourite song. Watch, notice and know that your words will have been heard.

Purpose of ritual: to commune with a dead loved one
What you need: your loved one's favourite fragrance or an essential oil of love, such as rose or lilac; a photograph of the person you want to contact; a tea-light and a holder; a soothing CD (optional)

- Go to your altar and set the oil burning. Light the illuminator candles and place the photograph on your altar where you can see it clearly. Light the tea-light and put it in front of the photo.
- Settle down and begin to talk to your loved one. Tell them why you wish to speak with them, what troubles you may be facing, what triumphs you've had and what you miss most about them. If tears come, don't worry, just let them flow, and pour out your heart.
- Once you have said all you wish to say, put on some soothing music, enjoy a warming drink and remain in your altar room until the tea-light has burned down. This can take up to five hours, so time your ritual carefully.

The Crone

I am the Crone,
I am the frost,
I am the realm where sunlight is lost.
I am the sorceress,
I am the dark,
I am the season that leaves death's mark.
I am the cold,
I am the snow,
I am the depths of the caverns below.
Mine is the wisdom
Of magic and spell;
I am the Goddess of secrets to tell.
Mine is the mystery,
The season of gloom;
I weave your destiny at the magical loom.
Mine is the step
That freezes the Earth;
I am the Goddess, awaiting rebirth.

November

The barren trees stand black and bare against a cold grey winter's sky. Each morning we awaken to a land of rain and frost. The temperature falls and the frozen earth slumbers, awaiting the first signs of distant spring. Winter has taken its grip on the land and we are now in the heart of the dark season. The once-crisp autumn leaves lie in a damp and sodden mulch, rotting into the ground, and we are reminded that what comes from the earth must once again return to the earth. Small children play in school playground puddles, the birds have migrated to warmer climes and much of our British wildlife is tucked away in hibernation.

It is now that we look to our inner selves, and many witches make full use of the dark season by beginning a course of magical book learning or developing a new skill.

The tree associated with November is the birch, or beith to the Celts, a tree of grace and longevity. Wiccans call the silver birch 'lady of the woods' and use its wood for sabbatic tools such as the Maypole and the Yule log. Broomsticks can also be made from birch wood, as the birch is considered to be a tree of cleansing and healing. Birch twigs can be carried by couples to aid fertility. The tree wisdom of the birch teaches us to have faith in ourselves, to be open to new projects and to be wise enough to know when to make a clean sweep. The birch dryad can help when we need to make a new start.

In the Victorian language of flowers, November's flower, the violet, stands for modesty and chastity. It is also a flower of self-love, so if you find yourself drawn to this little bloom you are being reminded to put yourself first occasionally and to nurture yourself.

The herbs of the month are cloves and sage. Sage is a herb of cleansing, and can be burnt on charcoal blocks, simmered in a pan or burnt as a smudge stick. Cloves are renowned for their ability to ease a toothache and can be added to food and punches.

November

Dawn 06.44
Dusk 16.43

Wednesday 1st

Moon quarter	2nd (waxing)	Crystal	Aventurine
Moon sign	♓	Sun sign	♏
Colour	Silver	Special	All Saints' Day
Herb or incense	Pine		

Thursday 2nd

Moon quarter	2nd (waxing)	Herb or incense	Borage
Moon sign	♓ 15.46 ♈	Crystal	Carnelian
Colour	Red	Sun sign	♏

Friday 3rd

Moon quarter	2nd (waxing)	Sun sign	♏
Moon sign	♈	Special	First recorded witch burning in Ireland (Patricia de Neath) 1605
Colour	Blue		
Herb or incense	Angelica		
Crystal	Snowy Quartz		

Saturday 4th

Moon quarter	2nd (waxing)	Herb or incense	Fennel
Moon sign	♈ 16.05 ♉	Crystal	Clear Quartz
Colour	Green	Sun sign	♏

Sunday 5th

Moon phase	○	Herb or incense	Bay
Time	12.58	Crystal	Snowflake-Obsidian
Moon quarter	3rd (waning)	Sun sign	♏
Moon sign	♉	Special	Snow Moon
Colour	Black		Guy Fawkes Day 1605

SNOW MOON

The full moon of November is known magically as the snow moon, so this would be the perfect time to invest in a snowflake-shaped lead crystal for your pendulum divinations.

Bonfire Night Sparkler Spell

During the all the celebrations of bonfire night, magic can be worked discreetly. This simple spell makes use of sparklers as a magical tool; you will need to buy them a week in advance. Choose any that appeal to you. Coloured sparklers would add the power of colour magic to your spell. You can repeat the spell as often as you like during the night. You can work with up to two goals in the same night – any more than that and your focus will not be strong enough.

Purpose of ritual: to empower a goal
What you need: a packet of sparklers, your pentacle

- Place the sparklers on your pentacle to charge for seven days.
- On the night of your bonfire celebrations, hold your hands over the sparklers, palms down, and say:

  I now dedicate these sparklers as a tool of power.
  May their magic burn bright this night. So be it!

- Take your sparklers outdoors and pick one to use. If you are using coloured sparklers, make sure the colour is conducive to your goal – green for prosperity, for example, or red for passion and love.
- Hold the sparkler in your hand. Close your eyes and concentrate on your magical goal. Once you are fully focused on your goal, light the sparkler and begin to spell out your goal with it.
- Once your sparkler has finished, dispose of it safely and carefully, observing fire precautions.

Guy Fawkes Spell

If you plan to burn a guy on bonfire night, then make him work for you! Fire magic is commonly used for banishings.

Purpose of spell: to cleanse your life of something that no longer serves you
What you need: the material for your guy, a handful of dried herbs suitable for banishing (such as hyssop, peppermint or tarragon), a slip of paper, a pen

- On the slip of paper write down what it is that you want to discard.

- As you create your effigy of Guy Fawkes, add the slip of paper and the handful of dried herbs. Finish stuffing and sewing your guy in the usual way and then sit him near your altar until bonfire night.
- On Guy Fawkes night, place the guy on your bonfire and ask him to take away whatever no longer serves you. When the fragrance of the herbs fills the air, your magic is in progress.

To Call Your Lover to You

Purpose of spell: to call your lover
What you need: five orange candles and appropriate holders, neroli essential oil, a brush, a photograph of your love and a lock of their hair, a slip of paper, a pen, your cauldron or a heatproof vessel, a lighter or matches

- Set out the candles in their holders to form the points of a pentagram big enough for you to sit within safely while you perform the spell.
- Once you are in the pentagram, paint your lover's name in neroli oil on each of the five candles. Light them all. Write the following charm on the slip of paper:

As these candles I now light
Within the darkness of the night,
Like a moth to a flame,
You will hear me call your name,
Drawing you near, Pulling you here,
Endlessly tied and bound.
By the strength of witch's charms,
I call you here into my arms.
I call down powers from above;
I chant the charm and spell my love,
Drawing you near, Pulling you here,
Soul mates forever found.

- Now speak the charm five times while focusing on the photograph.
- Place the lock of hair on the spell paper and roll it up in the form of a scroll. Light the end of the scroll from a candle and carefully drop it into the cauldron, allowing it to burn. The spell is now complete and your lover should be with you soon. You must remain within the pentagram until the candles have burnt out, so make sure you have a bottle of wine, nibbles and a good book.

November

Dawn 06.56
Dusk 16.31

Monday 6th

Moon quarter	3rd (waning)	Herb or incense	Lavender
Moon sign	♉ 16.46 ♊	Crystal	Kunzite
Colour	Yellow	Sun sign	♏

Tuesday 7th

Moon quarter	3rd (waning)	Herb or incense	Cinnamon
Moon sign	♊	Crystal	Amber
Colour	Indigo	Sun sign	♏

Wednesday 8th

Moon quarter	3rd (waning)	Herb or incense	Dill
Moon sign	♊ 19.46 ♋	Crystal	Red Jasper
Colour	Grey	Sun sign	♏

Thursday 9th

Moon quarter	3rd (waning)	Herb or incense	Catnip
Moon sign	♋	Crystal	Opal
Colour	Orange	Sun sign	♏

Friday 10th

Moon quarter	3rd (waning)	Herb or incense	Jasmine
Moon sign	♋	Crystal	Amethyst
Colour	Purple	Sun sign	♏

Saturday 11th

Moon quarter	3rd (waning)	Crystal	Bloodstone
Moon sign	♋ 02.34 ♌	Sun sign	♏
Colour	Red	Special	Armistice Day
Herb or incense	Frankincense		

Sunday 12th

Moon phase	◑	Colour	Jade
Time	17.45	Herb or incense	Parsley
Moon quarter	4th (waning)	Crystal	Jasper
Moon sign	♌	Sun sign	♏

November

Dawn 07.08
Dusk 16.21

Monday 13th			
Moon quarter	4th (waning)	Herb or incense	Mace
Moon sign	♌ 13.19 ♍	Crystal	Obsidian
Colour	Gold	Sun sign	♏

Tuesday 14th			
Moon quarter	4th (waning)	Herb or incense	Ginger
Moon sign	♍	Crystal	Citrine
Colour	Blue	Sun sign	♏

Wednesday 15th			
Moon quarter	4th (waning)	Herb or incense	Nutmeg
Moon sign	♍	Crystal	Hematite
Colour	White	Sun sign	♏

Thursday 16th			
Moon quarter	4th (waning)	Crystal	Rose Quartz
Moon sign	♍ 02.14 ♎	Sun sign	♏
Colour	Purple	Special	International Day of Tolerance
Herb or incense	Valerian		

Friday 17th			
Moon quarter	4th (waning)	Crystal	Moonstone
Moon sign	♎	Sun sign	♏
Colour	Green	Special	08.02 Venus ♀ enters Sagittarius ♐
Herb or incense	Lavender		

Saturday 18th			
Moon quarter	4th (waning)	Herb or incense	Jasmine
Moon sign	♎ 14.47 ♏	Crystal	Tiger's Eye
Colour	Green	Sun sign	♏

Sunday 19th			
Moon quarter	4th (waning)	Herb or incense	Dill
Moon sign	♏	Crystal	Jasper
Colour	Brown	Sun sign	♏

Automatic Writing

Automatic writing is a gentle way to contact the spirit world and carries none of the dangers of the ouija board. All you need is a pencil and a pad and a quiet space. If you like, you can meditate just prior to this exercise as a calm mind is very important. If you'd like to bring through a particular loved one's spirit, then focus on that person or meditate on their photograph.

Prepare your space in any way you like, lighting incense and maybe a couple of purple candles, then settle down comfortably. Hold the pencil very lightly in your fingers, place the point on the pad, relax and wait, keeping your focus on your aim for this automatic writing session. Eventually the pencil will begin to move, spelling out words or even drawing pictures.

If practised over a period of time, automatic writing gets easier. If you wish to practise this exercise regularly, buy an A4 blank book, maybe in a colour with spiritual associations, such as purple or indigo, to use for all your automatic writing sessions. You should first cleanse the book with incense smoke and dedicate it as your Spirit Book.

Ghost Hunting

As I mentioned earlier, during the darker months sightings of ghosts and ghostly phenomena increase, so you might like to take this opportunity to do a little ghost hunting! If you have an interest in ghosts and ghost sightings, this can be a great way to learn more and maybe even experience an encounter first hand.

Although the words 'ghost hunting' may bring a smile to your lips, they should be taken seriously. These are very real energies you are trying to connect with. If you know of any areas near your home that are reputed to be haunted, you might like to go along with a friend. At first you should visit in daylight. Record your feelings and what you felt the atmosphere was like. Then return to the same place by night and make a note of any changes – you could even visit at different phases of the moon to see if this has an effect on the atmosphere, your intuition or your psychic abilities. You might like to take a tape recorder, a camera or a camcorder with you, just in case!

A gentler form of ghost hunting, for those who are interested but faint of heart, is to collect books and stories about ghosts and hauntings in your area as there are many fascinating volumes available.

November

Dawn 07.18
Dusk 16.12

Monday 20th			
Moon phase	●	Colour	Silver
Time	22.18	Herb or incense	Mace
Moon quarter	1st (waxing)	Crystal	Moonstone
Moon sign	♏	Sun sign	♏

Tuesday 21st			
Moon quarter	1st (waxing)	Herb or incense	Catnip
Moon sign	♏ 01.15 ♐	Crystal	Rose Quartz
Colour	Red	Sun sign	♏

Wednesday 22nd			
Moon quarter	1st (waxing)	Herb or incense	Lavender
Moon sign	♐	Crystal	Topaz
Colour	Pink	Sun sign	♏ 11.02 ♐

Thursday 23rd			
Moon quarter	1st (waxing)	Herb or incense	Valerian
Moon sign	♐ 09.25 ♑	Crystal	Amethyst
Colour	Purple	Sun sign	♐

Friday 24th			
Moon quarter	1st (waxing)	Crystal	Opal
Moon sign	♑	Sun sign	♐
Colour	Blue	Special	04.43 Jupiter ♃ enters Sagittarius ♐
Herb or incense	Angelica		

Saturday 25th			
Moon quarter	1st (waxing)	Herb or incense	Sage
Moon sign	♑ 15.41 ♒	Crystal	Moonstone
Colour	Gold	Sun sign	♐

Sunday 26th			
Moon quarter	1st (waxing)	Herb or incense	Fennel
Moon sign	♒	Crystal	Carnelian
Colour	White	Sun sign	♐

November

Dawn 07.30 Dusk 16.05

Monday 27th

Moon quarter	1st (waxing)	Herb or incense	Cinnamon
Moon sign	♒ 20.21 ♓	Crystal	Amber
Colour	Green	Sun sign	♐

Tuesday 28th

Moon phase	◐	Colour	Pink
Time	06.29	Herb or incense	Ginger
Moon quarter	2nd (waxing)	Crystal	Citrine
Moon sign	♓	Sun sign	♐

Wednesday 29th

Moon quarter	2nd (waxing)	Herb or incense	Jasmine
Moon sign	♓ 23.30 ♈	Crystal	Jasper
Colour	Red	Sun sign	♐

Thursday 30th

Moon quarter	2nd (waxing)	Herb or incense	Thyme
Moon sign	♈	Crystal	Tiger's Eye
Colour	Silver	Sun sign	♐

SUN MOVES INTO SAGITTARIUS

The sun has now entered Sagittarius, the sign of the archer, represented by the magnificent centaur. Sagittarius is ruled by the planet Jupiter, ruler of all the gods. This is a very powerful sign, full of wisdom and understanding. The power stone is the sapphire and the birth stone is the amber topaz. Sagittarians are often very devoted to animals and will work diligently to protect and understand them.

They do have one weakness, which is that they can be quite judgemental and a little over-confident, which gives them an air of cockiness. At their best, however, they are very optimistic, kind, compassionate and open-minded.

Triple Circle-casting

The triple Circle is the strongest kind of Circle you can cast. There are many variations on casting it, and you may eventually create your own. Basically, the Circle is walked three times. On the first round, you hold out your athame/wand/finger in the usual way to perform the basic Circle-casting that by now you will be familiar with; on the second round you splash pure spring water around the Circle boundary to cleanse the space; and on the third and final walk you sprinkle sea salt around the boundary to define and protect the space.

This casting is very effective and powerful. You will be completely protected within the Circle. You should use it for all strong workings of protection magic.

Wiccan Winter Project

To a witch, the darker half of the year is a time of learning. During the long months of winter we set our minds to a course of study that will enhance and develop our magical skills and general awareness.

The subject of your winter project is entirely a matter of choice, but it should be connected with your magic in some way. For example, you might decide that you'd like to learn how to use the tarot or the Norse runes. Or maybe you'd like to study herbalism so that come spring you can create your own herb garden and potions. If you really can't think of a topic, try one of the following:

- Wicca
- Herbalism
- Aromatherapy
- North American shamanism
- Shape-shifting
- Divination (try to learn one particular tool, such as the tarot, etc.)
- Ghosts
- Psychic ability
- Dreams
- Mythology (focus on a particular culture or geographical area)
- Faery magic
- Dragon lore
- Candle rituals
- Celtic magic and spirituality
- Moon wisdom

- Crystals
- Astrology
- Astronomy
- Natural magic (sea, clouds, trees, rocks, etc.)
- Potions
- Mythical creatures

Your course of study should run from around October/November through to March, although you may choose to continue it through the summer months too. Whatever you decide to study, invest in new books and pens and a smart folder to keep your work in. Choose a colour to match your subject matter, for example green for the topic of herbalism, violet for psychic ability. Bear in mind any special tools you may need, such as tarot cards or a crystal ball. Visit bookstores and begin to create your own library of relevant books. If finances are a problem, then make full use of your local library's mind, body and spirit section.

Next, decide when you are going to study. How can you best fit your studies into your life? What other commitments do you have? How much time are you going to give to your project each week? When do you find study easiest – in the morning, on your day off, last thing at night? Are there any videos or audiotapes available that could assist you? Are there workshops at your local college? Will you study with a friend or alone?

Pick your subject, buy your stationery and begin your Wiccan project, going at your own pace.

Talking Candle

This is a form of fire scrying. You will need a natural beeswax candle in a sturdy holder. Place the candle on your altar and light it. The candle flame should be the only light in the room. Allow it to burn for a few moments and then begin to ask your questions. Make sure you only ask yes/no questions.

- If the candle flame gutters and jumps, the answer is positive.
- If it burns low or goes out, the answer is negative.
- If sparks fly from the flames, the outcome will be governed by an external force.

Thank the spirit of the flame, put out your candle and keep it solely for future scrying sessions.

Herne the Hunter

If the wildwood way you would come to learn
Step into the forest and call on Herne
Three times loud and three times clear
Then wait for a sign that Herne is near;
A shower of leaves though there is no breeze
Could be a message from the Lord of the Trees
And where two oaks stand tall and strong
The creak of the bark is the sound of his song
And there overhead a bare-branched bough
Could be the god of the antlered brow
Though darkness falls early and the forest seems dead
The rustle of bracken is his soft-booted tread
And we know he is here for he smells of the earth
As he carefully plants the seed of all birth
The cry of the wind is the sound of his horn
For he Masters the Wild Hunt and they ride out at dawn
And the rustle of leaves is the sound of his mirth
For he champions the Lady and they nurture the earth.

December

December is a hard cold month. The winter sunshine is watery and cool. Harsh winds blow, bringing a biting frost and sometimes ice and snows. In the hedgerows, deep red berries peek out from behind dark green holly leaves, mistletoe is brought into the house and a solitary robin chirps his thanks as he feasts at the bird-table.

Winter brings a season of darkness, but also a season of joy and light. Our homes are filled with glowing fires, flickering candles and twinkling fairy lights. We look forward to parties, theatre trips, pantomimes and ballets. When the snows come we may enjoy sledging and snowballing, or even just the sight of a white blanket covering the garden, unspoilt and pure. Late at night, the full moon shines on frost-covered trees, their branches sparkling. The winter landscape looks almost like fairyland, glittering with icicles and hoar frosts, when it is not swathed in freezing mists.

This is the time of the winter solstice – also known as Yule – and also of the Christian festival of Christmas. It is a season of gift-giving, blessings and good wishes, and of looking ahead to the new year.

In the Celtic Ogham, December is linked to the rowan tree, or luis. The rowan was believed to guard against witchcraft and to protect from enchantments. It was revered by the Druids, and also by the Vikings, who called it the runa, meaning 'charm tree'. The Vikings held the rowan sacred to Odin and also to Thor, two of their most powerful gods.

The pattern inside the rowan berry carries the symbol of the pentagram, the five-pointed star used in magic and witchcraft. It is traditionally believed that carrying a sprig of rowan will protect you from harm, and hanging one above the door to your house will protect and guard your home. Carrying a rowan walking stick is said to be sure protection while out walking at night, and a magical staff formed from rowan wood is extremely powerful. To find a rowan tree growing near a stone circle is said to be lucky, while if one grows on a ley line it is protected by dragon power and sacred to the dragon realm.

Another tree associated with the month of December is the yew, which is linked especially to the winter solstice, which occurs between December 19th and 23rd. The yew is an evergreen tree that bears orange-red berries during the autumn. It is extremely poisonous and must never be ingested. The yew tree is strongly associated with death. It is symbolic of the door of rebirth, probably because it is at its most beautiful during the autumn and winter, the seasons of death and rebirth.

The yew is also said to protect against ghosts, and it is for this reason that it is planted in graveyards and cemeteries throughout England and Scotland. (In Wales, the rowan tree is planted for this purpose, illustrating the links between the magical powers of these two trees.) To keep a sprig of yew in your home is traditionally believed to guard against hauntings, while it is said that if you stand beneath a yew tree in a graveyard you can safely communicate with the dead.

Both the rowan and the yew are steeped in legend and wisdom. Their dryads can be attuned with throughout the dark season.

The flower of December is the carnation, symbolising divine love. This connects the flower to the Goddess and to all divinity, as well as to the Christian celebration of Christmas. The herbs of December are patchouli and vervain, which can be mixed in equal parts and burnt as an incense at this time of year.

Cranberry and Popcorn Garlands

This is a rather festive way to decorate the garden and feed the birds over the festive season, and it's so simple you can get the kids involved.

You will need: strong string, cranberries, unsalted popcorn.

- Using strong twine or string, make a pretty garland of seasonal cranberries and unsalted popcorn. Make one very long garland or several smaller ones, and then take the finished garlands outside and use them to decorate the trees and shrubs in your garden.
- As you hang the garlands from the branches and boughs say the little blessing below:

'Seasonal garland bestowing good cheer
Feed the birds who spend winter here.
So mote it be.'

December

Dawn 07.30
Dusk 16.05

Friday 1st			
Moon quarter	2nd (waxing)	Herb or incense	Pine
Moon sign	♈	Crystal	Sodalite
Colour	Silver	Sun sign	♐

Saturday 2nd			
Moon quarter	2nd (waxing)	Herb or incense	Borage
Moon sign	♈ 01.26 ♉	Crystal	Jasper
Colour	Blue	Sun sign	♐

Sunday 3rd			
Moon quarter	2nd (waxing)	Herb or incense	Fennel
Moon sign	♉	Crystal	Tiger's Eye
Colour	Purple	Sun sign	♐

Magical Mistletoe

Mistletoe is also called the Golden Bough. It is a plant that has long been associated with magic and paganism, particularly Druidry, and was considered to be especially sacred if found growing in an oak tree.

Tradition states that it should only be cut with a golden sickle and that it should not be allowed to touch the floor – hence it is caught in a white altar cloth and held aloft by the druids or coven members. Its white berries are said to be the seed of the pagan god and so the plant is associated with fertility and sexuality. To kiss beneath the mistletoe is said to bring luck, blessings and longevity to your relationship.

Mistletoe is also associated with healing, protection and general good luck. In the past it was believed that to wear a mistletoe garland around the neck would render the wearer invisible. It was also thought to protect against lightning.

Mistletoe is an extremely magical plant and hanging it in the house during the festive season is an old tradition. However, witches tend to keep their mistletoe all year round, allowing it to dry and so keeping love, luck and blessings flowing into the house. Replace your mistletoe each Yuletide, putting the old bough into the garden and so giving it back to the earth, or grind it up and use it in magical spell powders or incenses.

December

Dawn 07.39
Dusk 16.00

Monday 4th			
Moon quarter	2nd (waxing)	Herb or incense	Thyme
Moon sign	♉ 03.05 ♊	Crystal	Hematite
Colour	Indigo	Sun sign	♐

Tuesday 5th			
Moon phase	○	Herb or incense	Rosemary
Time	00.25	Crystal	Moonstone
Moon quarter	3rd (waning)	Sun sign	♐
Moon sign	♊	Special	Oak Moon
Colour	Orange		

Wednesday 6th			
Moon quarter	3rd (waning)	Crystal	Rose Quartz
Moon sign	♊ 06.00 ♋	Sun sign	♐
Colour	Green	Special	04.58 Mars ♂ enters Sagittarius ♐
Herb or incense	Jasmine		

Thursday 7th			
Moon quarter	3rd (waning)	Herb or incense	Ginger
Moon sign	♋	Crystal	Clear Quartz
Colour	Pink	Sun sign	♐

Friday 8th			
Moon quarter	3rd (waning)	Crystal	Aventurine
Moon sign	♋ 11.52 ♌	Sun sign	♐
Colour	Purple	Special	05.52 Mercury ☿ enters Sagittarius ♐
Herb or incense	Catnip		

Saturday 9th			
Moon quarter	3rd (waning)	Herb or incense	Mugwort
Moon sign	♌	Crystal	Bloodstone
Colour	Jade	Sun sign	♐

Sunday 10th			
Moon quarter	3rd (waning)	Crystal	Clear Quartz
Moon sign	♌ 21.31 ♍	Sun sign	♐
Colour	Yellow	Special	Human Rights Day
Herb or incense	Bayberry		

OAK MOON

December's full moon is known as the oak moon, once again reminding us that the Oak King is back and the light half of the year will soon be with us. The wheel has turned.

Spell for Religious Understanding

Purpose of spell: to enhance understanding between all the world religions

What you need: a white candle and a holder

- Holding the candle in your hands, empower it with the desire for love and understanding between all the religions of the world.
- Place the candle in a sturdy holder on your altar, light it and begin the chant:

All Gods are one God;
Let people see,
All Gods are one God.
So mote it be!

- Continue to chant for as long as you comfortably can. Allow the candle to burn down naturally, keeping a close eye on it at all times.

December

Dawn 07.47
Dusk 15.58

Monday 11th

Moon quarter	3rd (waning)	Crystal	Amber
Moon sign	♍	Sun sign	♐
Colour	Grey	Special	05.33 Venus ♀
Herb or incense	Mint		enters Capricorn ♑

Tuesday 12th

Moon phase	◑	Colour	Blue
Time	14.32	Herb or incense	Dill
Moon quarter	4th (waning)	Crystal	Red Jasper
Moon sign	♍	Sun sign	♐

Wednesday 13th

Moon quarter	4th (waning)	Herb or incense	Sage
Moon sign	♍ 10.00 ♎	Crystal	Carnelian
Colour	Red	Sun sign	♐

Thursday 14th

Moon quarter	4th (waning)	Herb or incense	Mace
Moon sign	♎	Crystal	Topaz
Colour	Brown	Sun sign	♐

Friday 15th

Moon quarter	4th (waning)	Herb or incense	Angelica
Moon sign	♎ 22.43 ♏	Crystal	Kunzite
Colour	Peach	Sun sign	♐

Saturday 16th

Moon quarter	4th (waning)	Herb or incense	Nutmeg
Moon sign	♏	Crystal	Smokey Quartz
Colour	Indigo	Sun sign	♐

Sunday 17th

Moon quarter	4th (waning)	Crystal	Citrine
Moon sign	♏	Sun sign	♐
Colour	White	Special	Saturnalia (Ancient
Herb or incense	Cinnamon		Roman festival)

Herne the Hunter Shrine

When I think of the Yuletide season, I think of stags, reindeer and elk. These are animals that are associated with snowy climes, and, being antlered beasts, they are also sacred to Herne the Hunter. Herne is an aspect of the witches' God, and as he exists in the woods he is another face of the Green Man.

December and the winter solstice are Herne's time, and many Wiccans choose to attune with him during their solstice celebrations and throughout this month. The best way to do this is to create a little altar dedicated to him. This can be as simple as adapting your existing Green Man altar to represent the hunter, or you might like to create a separate shrine elsewhere in your home.

Choose a brown altar cloth and be imaginative with your candle holders – these days we are spoilt for choice. On a simple altar you could use two wooden candle sticks, while a more complex altar might include candle sticks fashioned to look like small trees – remember that Herne is Lord of the Greenwood. You could also include a set of antlers or an antler-handled hunting knife. Because Herne was the leader of the Wild Hunt, bringing the depths of winter in his wake, you could also add a small hunting horn, black horses, hunting hounds and so on. In a central place on your altar you should place a figure to represent Herne. This could be a statue of Herne himself (though these can be expensive) or you could use a figure of a deer, stag or reindeer, which can be bought quite cheaply at this time of year.

I have two wonderful stag figures whose silver antlers are designed to hold a tall dinner candle. One stag is prancing, the other is lying down. Such things are out there – you only have to look, remain focused on what you want and it will come to you. You can also buy large stags whose antlers will hold many tea-lights – one of these would be a shrine in itself! Don't forget garden centres, where you may pick up a bargain deer or stag during the colder months.

Once you are all set up, burn a winter oil at your altar every day and attune with the great hunter.

December

Dawn 07.53
Dusk 15.59

Monday 18th

Moon quarter	4th (waning)	Herb or incense	Parsley
Moon sign	♏ 09.10 ♐	Crystal	Amethyst
Colour	Gold	Sun sign	♐

Tuesday 19th

Moon quarter	4th (waning)	Herb or incense	Pine
Moon sign	♐	Crystal	Sodalite
Colour	Yellow	Sun sign	♐

Wednesday 20th

Moon phase	●	Colour	Green
Time	14.01	Herb or incense	Valerian
Moon quarter	1st (waxing)	Crystal	Aventurine
Moon sign	♐ 16.39 ♑	Sun sign	♐

Thursday 21st

Moon quarter	1st (waxing)	Herb or incense	Bayberry
Moon sign	♑	Crystal	Snowy Quartz
Colour	Red	Sun sign	♐

Friday 22nd

Moon quarter	1st (waxing)	Crystal	Snowflake-Obsidian
Moon sign	♑ 21.49 ♒	Sun sign	♐ 00.22 ♑
Colour	Silver	Special	Yule (winter solstice 00.22)
Herb or incense	Pine		

Saturday 23rd

Moon quarter	1st (waxing)	Herb or incense	Cinnamon
Moon sign	♒	Crystal	Topaz
Colour	Green	Sun sign	♑

Sunday 24th

Moon quarter	1st (waxing)	Herb or incense	Ginger
Moon sign	♒	Crystal	Red Jasper
Colour	White	Sun sign	♑

SUN MOVES INTO CAPRICORN

On December 22nd, the sun enters the sign of Capricorn, which is ruled by the planet Saturn. Capricorn's birth stone is turquoise and its power stone is jet. Capricorn is a sign of ambition and integrity, and those born under it will have a tendency to be absorbed in their own status. They are eager to appear successful to the outside world.

On the negative side, Capricorns can be slightly manipulative and a bit snobbish, but at their best they are dependable and hard-working individuals who strive to excel.

YULE

Yule is the sabbat of the winter solstice. This is the longest night, when we enjoy more than 12 hours of darkness as we wait for the dawn. Yule is a celebration of the rebirth of the sun, for now that the longest night is here, the sun will again begin to grow stronger. This time the Oak King prevails over the Holly King, to bring us the light half of the year.

The tradition of a mid-winter festival is ancient, as the celebration helps the long winter to pass and gives us something to look forward to. Yule is a time of sparkling frosts and snows, evergreens and red berries, and we try to echo this in our ritual decorations. A traditional altar set-up will have a green altar cloth and red candles; holly, ivy and mistletoe will be used, and candle holders that are painted with holly leaves are also appropriate. A sprinkling of berries could be added and perhaps a statue or figure of something that represents the season – a stag, an angel or a miniature Yuletide tree for example.

If you fancy a more modern Yuletide altar, here are some ideas. Drape your altar with a white, silver or ice-blue satin cloth. Sprinkle snowflake confetti all over the surface. Add two silver candles, preferably set in silver candle sticks, or use tea-lights in holders of a snowflake design. Hang sparkling glass icicles from the altar cloth to form a trim. Spray fallen twigs silver and arrange them in a silver or white vase. Spray pine cones silver too, sprinkle them with silver glitter and place them in a crystal bowl. Finally, add a silver angel, an ice maiden or a snow queen figure to the centre.

Whichever type of altar you choose, make sure you add your Prosperity Yule Candle and light it at dusk. Your ritual celebrations could include decorating the Yuletide tree, carol singing, a party, a seasonal film such as *Box of Delights,* a winter walk, a gathering of Wiccan friends and so on. Gift-giving is traditional at this time, as is the long vigil to see the dawn and the rebirth of the sun. You could do this alone in your garden, from a local hilltop or with Pagan friends.

Sometimes local covens organise an open Yule ritual, which anyone interested can take part in. If so, don't be afraid to join in and talk to like-minded people. But, of course, it's equally okay to celebrate the sabbat in your own way, writing a ritual that really means something to you.

Afterwards, settle down to your ritual feast. Traditional foods include joints of meat, stews and casseroles, chestnut stuffing, roast chestnuts, cinnamon cakes, nuts, plum pudding and, of course, the chocolate Yule log – okay, so the last one's not exactly traditional, but it's good to indulge once in a while! Wassail, however, is a traditional drink. It is apple based, rather like the mulled ciders and wines that these days can be bought ready made from most off-licences and some supermarkets. Eggnog, too, is very appropriate (and my favourite), though it's a little too sticky for a libation!

Prosperity Yule Candle

Yule is an excellent time to perform a prosperity spell to help ensure abundance through the remainder of the dark season. In these days of gas fires and central heating, it is also a good way of keeping the spirit of the Yule log tradition alive.

Purpose of spell: to ensure abundance through the winter

What you need: a large, fat, deep-red church candle (to represent the sun) and a gold-coloured candle platter; a packet of bayberry incense sticks; bayberry essential oil; a paint brush; a few holly sprigs

- Take all the items to your altar and light the bayberry incense.
- Paint the candle generously with the bayberry oil, at the same time visualising prosperity coming to you from all sides.
- Place the anointed candle on the gold platter and arrange the sprigs of holly around the base. Leave it on your altar until the night of the winter solstice, when it will form a part of your Yuletide altar set-up and will be burnt during the sabbat.

Elf Song Spell for Christmas Eve

On the night known as Christmas eve, the world is hushed and still. It is a magical night, regardless of your religious beliefs, as the world is caught up in mid-winter merry-making. Of course, for children this is the night when Santa brings their gifts, aided by his faithful elves!

Magically speaking, the elves are actually a form of elemental. Like the dryads, they are attached to woodlands, although they are not connected to any particular tree. They simply wander the woods and forests and indulge in crafts, making things of exquisite beauty. One of the most beautiful representations of elves that I have come across, is in the film *Fellowship of the Ring,* the first in the *Lord of the Rings* trilogy. Here the elves are tall, willowy and very magical.

At this time of the year, we are more open to the magic of the elves, and we can connect with these very real elementals by performing this ritual. If you like, you could go for a winter walk and perform the ritual in a nearby woodland, attuning with the elves on their own ground.

Purpose of ritual: to connect with the elves
What you need: a figure, picture or other object to symbolise the elves; a silver candle

- Place your symbol of the elves on the Yuletide altar. Light a silver candle and begin to chant this elf song:

Elven ones of grace so rare,
Of gentle eyes and golden hair,
Skilled in herb, wood and metal,
Seeing wisdom in each unfolding petal,
Who know the teachings of the stars,
May your friendship soon be ours.
And in the woods at dead of night,
Elven Lords may come in sight.
And on the wind at break of day,
You may hear a whisper say:
'Treat all nature with respect,
Or our teachings you reject.
Learn from beast, bud and leaf;
Give thanks for every golden sheaf.
Hear now the wisdom of the Elves,
Put love of nature before yourselves.'
Elven ones of grace so rare,

Of gentle eyes and golden hair,
With open heart I stand before thee;
I open my mind to all you teach me.
In love and trust these words I send
And welcome the love of an Elven friend.

- Once you have spoken the charm, give an offering to the earth. Repeat this ritual as often as you like. Eventually you will receive a sign that the elves have accepted your friendship.

CHRISTMAS DAY

Today is celebrated throughout the Christian world as Christmas day. Christmas plays such a huge role in modern society that it would be difficult to turn away from it altogether, and so many Pagans celebrate one long winter festival in order to please more orthodox relatives. (As you will have noticed, many Christian and Pagan festivals are very similar anyway, due to the absorption of Pagan traditions into early Christianity.) There is nothing wrong with taking part in Christmas, and it doesn't make you less Pagan. Just make sure your main spiritual festival is on Yuletide and then party on!

Spell to Bless a New Diary

New Year's Eve is the perfect time to bless your new diary for the coming year. Take the diary to your altar and light the illuminator candles. Take also a pen, a bottle of your favourite essential oil and a cotton wool pad.

Sit quietly for a moment and breathe deeply until you are centred. Now hold your new diary in your hands and close your eyes. Imagine yourself writing the diary, filling each page with positive thoughts, feelings and incidents. See yourself smiling as you write. Now repeat the chant below nine times:

'As my life moves forward through the ages
May all good things fill these pages.'

Next pour a few drops of essential oil on to the cotton pad and rub it over the covers of the diary, maintaining the visualisation as you do so. Finally write the chant above on to the first page of the diary to complete the blessing. Leave the diary on your altar until you make your first entry on New Year's Day. Blow out the candles and enjoy this special night. Happy New Year!

December

Dawn 07.59
Dusk 16.07

Monday 25th

Moon quarter	1st (waxing)	Crystal	Aventurine
Moon sign	♒ 10.17 ♓	Sun sign	♑
Colour	Gold	Special	Christmas Day
Herb or incense	Frankincense		

Tuesday 26th

Moon quarter	1st (waxing)	Herb or incense	Pine
Moon sign	♓	Crystal	Tiger's Eye
Colour	Blue	Sun sign	♑

Wednesday 27th

Moon phase	◐	Herb or incense	Nutmeg
Time	14.48	Crystal	Rose Quartz
Moon quarter	2nd (waxing)	Sun sign	♑
Moon sign	♓ 05.04 ♈	Special	20.55 Mercury ☿ enters Capricorn ♑
Colour	Orange		

Thursday 28th

Moon quarter	2nd (waxing)	Herb or incense	Angelica
Moon sign	♈	Crystal	Moonstone
Colour	Purple	Sun sign	♑

Friday 29th

Moon quarter	2nd (waxing)	Herb or incense	Mace
Moon sign	♈ 08.08 ♉	Crystal	Carnelian
Colour	Pink	Sun sign	♑

Saturday 30th

Moon quarter	2nd (waxing)	Herb or incense	Fennel
Moon sign	♉	Crystal	Amethyst
Colour	White	Sun sign	♑

Sunday 31st

Moon quarter	2nd (waxing)	Crystal	Snowy Quartz
Moon sign	♉ 11.16 ♊	Sun sign	♑
Colour	Silver	Special	New Year's Eve
Herb or incense	Ginger		

Afterword

Well, that's that – the end of the year and the end of the book. I hope that you have enjoyed your journey through the seasons with me, and that you have comes across spells and rituals to interest and inspire you. I have deliberately avoided giving set rituals for every one of the sabbats, as I feel that the wheel of the year should be celebrated in an individual way. Instead, I have included one or two for you to use as a blueprint for your own sabbatic rituals.

Having looked at the magic and wisdom of trees, stags, wolves, dragons, angels, faeries, gods, goddesses and elves, hopefully you will now feel ready to try out some of the spells in this book, and to have a go at writing your own rituals.

Remember that the key to magic lies in nature, in the world around us and in you yourself. You are an Earth child, a walker of the Old Ways and a daughter/son of the Great Goddess. Knowing this, you will realise that magic is all around you on a daily basis and the power to change your life for the better is at your fingertips. Enjoy your magic, use your power wisely and celebrate the sabbats in a way that makes a statement about who you are. Farewell my magical reader. May your gods go with you, until our next merry meeting!

Bright blessings be upon you!

Morgana

Index

Further Reading

All these titles are published by Foulsham/Quantum and are available from good bookshops or direct from www.foulsham.com.

Bruce, Marie, *Candleburning Rituals,* 0-572-02692-7
Bruce, Marie, *Everyday Spells for a Teenage Witch,* 0-572-02770-2
Bruce, Marie, *Faerie Magick,* 0-572-03123-8
Bruce, Marie, *First Steps to Solitary Witchcraft,* 0-572-03068-1
Bruce, Marie, *How to Create a Magical Home,* 0-572-02963-2
Bruce, Marie, *Magical Beasts,* 0-572-02928-4
Eason, Cassandra, *Complete Book of Spells,* 0-572-03001-0
Eason, Cassandra, *Crystals Talk to the Woman Within,* 0-572-02613-7
Eason, Cassandra, *Every Woman a Witch,* 0-572-02223-9
Eason, Cassandra, *Fragrant Magic,* 0-572-02939-X
Eason, Cassanda, *Magic Spells for a Happy Life,* 0-572-02827-X
Eason, Cassandra, *A Practical Guide to Witchcraft and Magick Spells,* 0-572-02704-4
Kollerstrom, Nick, *Gardening and Planting by the Moon* 2006, 0-572-03132-7
Page, James Lynn, *Celtic Magic,* 0-572-02736-2
Page, James Lynn, *Native American Magic,* 0-572-02740-0
Rodway, Marie, *A Wiccan Herbal,* 0-572-02340-5